P9-DGC-185

GOD'S WORD
in its FULLNESS

GOD'S WORD
in its FULLNESS

DR. TIMOTHY F. NEU

XULON PRESS

Xulon Press
2301 Lucien Way #415
Maitland, FL 32751
407.339.4217
www.xulonpress.com

© 2018 by Dr. Timothy F. Neu

All rights reserved solely by the author. The author guarantees all contents are original and do not infringe upon the legal rights of any other person or work. No part of this book may be reproduced in any form without the permission of the author. The views expressed in this book are not necessarily those of the publisher.

Unless otherwise indicated, Scripture quotations taken from The Holy Bible: International Standard Version. Release 2.0, Build 2015.02.09. Copyright © 1995-2014 by ISV Foundation. ALL RIGHTS RESERVED INTERNATIONALLY. Used by permission of Davidson Press, LLC.

Scripture quotations taken from the King James Version (KJV)— *public domain.*

Scripture quotations taken from the Holy Bible, New International Version (NIV). Copyright © 1973, 1978, 1984, 2011 by Biblica, Inc.™. Used by permission. All rights reserved.

Printed in the United States of America.

ISBN-13: 9781545641323

Table of Contents

Introduction. vii
Dedication. xi
Acknowledgements. xiii
Endorsements xv

Chapter One   The Journey Begins. 1
Chapter Two   How Firm A Foundation 11
Chapter Three   Preacher Boy 19
Chapter Four   You're Too Young 27
Chapter Five   In Sickness and Health 35
Chapter Six   Obey All Things 43
Chapter Seven   Ministry Detour. 51
Chapter Eight   Give Thanks. 59
Chapter Nine   Lessons in Leadership 69
Chapter Ten   Empowering Churches 79
Chapter Eleven   All Things 89
Chapter Twelve   A Sense of Urgency. 97
Chapter Thirteen   Scriptures Make a Difference 105
Chapter Fourteen   Entrusting the Faithful. 113

About the Author. 123

Introduction

Verse

*...by the commission God gave me to present to you the Word of God
in its fullness...so that we may present everyone perfect in Christ.
Colossians 1:25, 28*

Growing up, I enjoyed listening to music probably because most
of my family were into one form of music or another. Saturday nights at
one grandparent's house Lawrence Welk and at the other was Hee-Haw.
Riding in the car with my dad, we sang along with the radio or 8-trak
playing country. At home with my mom, we stacked up the 45s and
played old time rock-n-roll. I liked it all! Some of my favorite artists were
Anne Murray, Barbara Mandrell, Elvis, The Eagles, and The Guess Who.

By the time I was a teen, I had settled into 70s and 80s rock. I loved
the sounds of Boston, Styx, Journey and several others—even a couple
of metal bands. My grandma would say, "It's a bunch of noise! You can't
even understand the words!" I didn't care much about the words back
then. The tunes were catchy, and I liked them.

When I enrolled in Bible school, I signed the student handbook
agreeing that I wouldn't listen to secular music while I was at school.
Some of my classmates read that portion of the handbook quite literally.
They never listened to secular music on campus. But you could hear the
rock-n-roll music cranked as they pulled away from the parking lot. I had
decided to set aside the secular music for that season. Instead, I picked
up some cassette tapes with Christian artists like Steve Green, Steve and
Annie Chapman, Twila Paris, and Glad. And their songs became my new
favorites.

I didn't know it then, but God would allow me to be involved in the music ministry at a local Church. A friend would teach me how to play guitar which led to playing music in the worship service. Eventually, I became the choir director. I loved listening to the songs in preparation and picking the cantatas each year. Every time I introduced a new piece to the group, I'd say, "You guys are going to love this one! It's my favorite song!"

"Tim, every song is your favorite song." One of my buddies would say.

"I know. But today, this is my favorite." I would answer. After a while, I would simply start out, "And this is my..."

"Favorite song!" Everyone in the choir would respond.

The routine with my favorite songs in choir carried over into my teaching with the youth. Just like favorite songs, I had favorite verses. It didn't take long before the group started responding like the choir. The setting made no difference. Whether in Sunday school or morning service, whenever I said, "This is one of my..." the group would finish the statement with "...favorite verses."

I've had several favorite verses over the years. But as I neared the age of 50, one verse stood out to me in a way that I had never seen before. I was reading Paul's letter to the Church at Colosse. Early in the letter, Paul said, "...since the day we heard about you, we have not stopped praying for you and asking God to fill you with the knowledge of his will through all spiritual wisdom and understanding." I remember thinking, *what an amazing prayer. God, I want to be filled with the knowledge of Your will with all spiritual wisdom and understanding*. The letter continued, "And we pray this in order that you may live a life worthy of the Lord and may please him in every way..." For some reason, my emotions were being stirred as I read. I was thinking to myself, *Yes Lord. I want to live a worthy life. I want to please You in every way.*

Just a few verses later, Paul said, "...by the commission God gave me to present to you the Word of God in its fullness...so that we may present everyone perfect in Christ." And there it was! Something I had never seen before! Paul just declared his life's purpose—his mission statement! Questions immediately flooded my mind. *What's my life's purpose? What's my mission statement? What do I want to be known and remembered for?* And *why didn't I see this before?*

I cannot recount the number of times I've read this passage of Scripture. It shouldn't have been a surprise that God would reveal something new from this or any passage. If God's mercies are new every morning and His Word is alive and active, then of course I'm going to see things in Scripture that I haven't seen before. In this moment, I was finally in a place that I could hear the Holy Spirit saying, *take note! This is a worthy life's purpose!*

We can see through other passages in Scripture that Paul was uniquely prepared by God for this purpose to present God's Word in its fullness. In the pages that follow, I will share how God has worked in my life to prepare me to do the same—present God's Word in its fullness.

Dedication

This book is dedicated to my lovely wife, Nancy, and daughters Sarah, and Stephanie. Without them, I would not be the man I am today.

Nancy, you've known me the longest and know me the best. And, still you love me. I am truly blessed. Thank you for sharing life with me. Thank you for enduring this season of busyness as I have spent so many hours at my desk studying and writing. Your love and support mean the world to me.

Sarah and Stephanie, I prayed that God would give me girls and He gave me you two. You have brought love and joy to my life that I never could have imagined. It has been a great honor for me to be your dad. I pray that you continue to pursue God and receive His Word in its fullness. And in doing so, you will be the helpers together with your husbands in passing on His Word in its fullness to your children and their children.

Acknowledgements

Verse

*You show that you are a letter from Christ, the result of our ministry,
written not with ink but with the Spirit of the living God, not on tablets
of stone but on tablets of human hearts. 2 Corinthians 3:3*

Pastor Mark Benson, a good friend and mentor of mine, was
asked years ago, "How long did it take you to prepare that message?" His
response, "It took a lifetime." I found the answer peculiar when I heard it.
But I remembered those words as I wrote this book. The lessons I share
in the pages that follow have taken a lifetime to learn. In fact, I'm still
learning as God patiently writes His Word on my heart by His Spirit and
through the faithful input of others.

This book would not have been possible without the faithful input
of others.

Bruce Smith, my boss and mentor, has faithfully encouraged and
supported me on my professional development—from acquiring my CPA
license to completing a PhD in Biblical studies. His words of encouragement have inspired me every step of the way. When he suggested I
write this book, I must admit it felt like a tall task. Bruce, thank you for
inviting me to be part of an amazing team and for seeing more in me
than I could see myself. Thanks especially for making it possible to serve
in ways that God has gifted me and to do things within the passions He
placed in my heart.

When my colleague and friend, Frank Nolan, heard that I was possibly writing a book, he suggested a broader audience would be interested—more than my family and close friends. He encouraged me to get
started right away providing input and support as I wrote. Frank, thank

you for the encouragement that others would benefit from reading my story. Thanks too for taking time to read my manuscript and providing valuable input along the way.

Tabitha Price spent countless hours reviewing and editing the pages of this book. As an experienced author and editor, she knew the right questions to ask and suggestions to make. Tabitha, thank you for patiently working with me. Your comments and encouragement made this writing experience a joy.

Cindy Gray read some of the earliest drafts of my book in order to design the cover. Cindy, thank you for reading the earliest manuscripts. And, for lending your creative talent and art work. I loved all of the designs you prepared.

My lovely wife, Nancy, put up with long hours of alone time while I worked on this book. She also invested hours of time proofreading and providing input with each chapter. Sweetheart, thank you for tolerating the long weekends and evenings while I was holed up in the office writing. Thank you too for allowing me to share some of the difficult times we have faced over the years. Your love and support mean the world to me.

Several family members read the early drafts and provided feedback—my mom, daughters Sarah and Stephanie, and parents-in-law Neal and Carol. Thank you all for reading and reminiscing with me as you read through the pages. Thanks for the encouragement to see this project through to completion and for letting me include life experiences that we have shared together.

Finally, I want to thank my many friends at Ethnos360 (formerly New Tribes Mission) and Wycliffe Associates. Your example of Christ's life and love have forever influenced me. You and so many others over the years have been God's writing instrument as He penned the fullness of His Word in my heart. I pray that we will all continue ministering as God's instruments in writing His Word in its fullness on the hearts of others.

Endorsements

"During four decades of international ministry, I've been blessed to work with many of God's humble servants. Tim is one of these. His professional commitment, ministry experience, and personal character have strengthened the Wycliffe Associates team and overflowed as blessings to millions of people who now have Scripture in their heart language as a result. Tim's accounts of God shaping him throughout his lifetime reflect a man anxious to be molded by the Master's hands. I'm blessed by Tim's testimony and encouragement, and I know you will be blessed by these as well."

  Dr. Bruce A. Smith
  President and CEO
  Wycliffe Associates

"Tim Neu is the kind of inspiring person that people want to be around and to emulate. You can spend five minutes with Tim and know that he is a gifted yet humble man who truly seeks to follow and do the will of God in all he does. This book, God's Word in Its Fullness, engagingly ushers the reader through a tapestry of callings, challenges, opportunities, pain, and great joy…and helps the reader understand in a deeply personal and authentic way the source of true joy. Tim helps us realize, through vivid illustration, that God has a plan…and it is a good plan. It is remarkable to see how He has demonstrated that so clearly in Tim's life as now shared through this uplifting book."

  Michael E. Batts, CPA
  President and Managing Partner
  Batts Morrison Wales & Lee
  Certified Public Accountants

This book is a delight to read and devotional in its spiritual depth. Tim Neu is a master storyteller along with being a pioneer in the Kingdom. I loved how he weaves personal stories with the Gospel's calling and Biblical principles. It will open your eyes to the larger picture of what God is doing in these days!

Dr. Joel C. Hunter, Faith Community Organizer
Chair, Central Florida Commission on Homelessness
Chair, Community Resource Network
Chair, Slingshot (a micro-church network)

"A well-written and insightful presentation of how the Lord has led his servant from those formative years in Michigan through more than thirty years of training and ministry. Tim's love and burden for Bible translation is truly an inspiration."

Dr. David Keeny
Dean of Biblical Studies
Louisiana Baptist University

"Tim has prepared an easy read that outlines a heartfelt, sad beginning and culminates in how God worked to produce extraordinary results. This book is a picture of trusting and believing what God says and overcoming to an incredible level."

Scott K. Ross, Esq.
House Counsel (Retired)
Ethnos360

Chapter One

The Journey Begins

Verse

For God so loved the world, that He gave His only begotten Son, that whosoever believeth in Him should not perish, but have everlasting life.
John 3:16 KJV

Introduction

When we meet someone for the first time, we often get the conversation started by introducing ourselves and asking, "So, where are you from?" Some will answer with their home town. Others will mention their home state or a combination of both. It is especially fun when we recognize the place because we've either been there or know someone who lives nearby. On occasion, I've had to admit that I'm not familiar with that part of the country or State. Most of the time, folks mention a more commonly known town in the general vicinity. But occasionally, they respond with an equally obscure town which results in one of two things. I either give them the puzzled look indicating *I still have no idea where that is located,* or I simply nod and politely move on to another topic.

I grew up in Michigan (MI). So, when people ask, "Tim, where are you from?" I have no trouble at all telling them because everyone from MI carries a state map everywhere they go. It's quite handy. I was born in Lansing and grew up in Jackson. To show a new friend where this is, I might hold up my right hand with the palm facing out and point at a spot in the middle of my palm close to the bottom of my hand. It's important to get these details correct. I would have chosen my right hand with the palm facing out so that folks would see the MI mitten properly oriented.

When I was growing up, Jackson was known for being the home of the Cascades water falls, Jackson All-star Dairy (Lowds), and MI State Penitentiary (Cooper St. College). Sadly, the penitentiary was likely the most well-known of the places mentioned. Some other interesting factoids about Jackson are, that it was the birth place of the Republican party, the city where Jack Parr a famous tonight show host grew up, and the place Tony Dungy, one of the NFL's great coaches, called home.

Some might suggest it is a good place to be from with emphasis on the *from*. For me, it is still my home town. I have fond memories of growing up in Jackson; playing t-ball and recreation soccer, riding bikes, and hanging out with my friends. It's where I went to school, met the girl who became my wife, and most importantly where my spiritual journey began when I heard these words for the first time, "For God so loved the world, that He gave His only begotten Son."

Smelt and Mixed Veggies

However, not all my growing up memories in Jackson were so great. As is true for all kids, there were what I will refer to as learning opportunities that usually involved some form of discipline. For me, it was most often a spanking. To be sure, I never liked getting a spanking, but I appreciated the fact that it was generally quick and final. Occasionally, there was the added two weeks of being grounded which really put a crimp in my after-school play time with friends. I could generally tell if there was going to be the bonus grounding period. There was a certain tone in mom's voice as she called out my name, TIMOTHY FOREST NEU. Pretty much everyone in proximity knew something serious was about to happen. I heard that call most often in the evenings after the street light out in front of our house lit up. The rule was simple enough to understand. Mom was clear when she said, "Tim, you are to be back in the house before dark. That means when the street light comes on."

"Okay. Got it mom." I'd say as I rushed out the door.

"Remember! When the street light comes on—back in the house." She often said a second time.

"Yep! I got it. When the street light is on." It wasn't even a bad rule because that was about the time the mosquitos started biting and I didn't want to be outside anyway. The problem is that the street light was in front of our house. My friends and I rarely played where you could see that crazy light. We were most often playing ball down the street or in one

2

of our back yards. Needless to say, that light became a sore spot between mom and me, mostly for me, for a long time.

But those disciplines weren't so bad. Those learning opportunities bring a smile to my face. The memories that aren't so great, generally relate to my mom and dad's divorce. I was quite little at the time and really didn't know what was happening except that one day it was just mom and me. Occasionally, I would go stay with my dad on the weekend. I remember one special meeting that mom, dad and I went to down town. It was in one of the older buildings and it was with an older man who looked very official. The older man invited me into his office all by myself. When the door closed, and we made ourselves comfortable in chairs near his desk, he began asking the most unusual questions. "So, Tim, is it okay if I call you Tim or do you go by Timothy?"

"Tim is ok." I said.

"You probably love your mom and dad very much, don't you?" He asked.

"Yes sir. I do." I replied.

"Do you know why we are meeting today?" He asked.

"I guess so." I said not really knowing much other than mom and dad didn't seem happy when we were together.

"Well, your mom and dad will not be living in the same house any-more. And, we are here today to decide where you are going to live. Who would you like to live with? Your mom or your dad?" He asked.

What kind of question was that to ask someone who just started kindergarten? "Both!" I answered. He went on to let me know that this wasn't an option. So, I told him that I wanted to live with my mom. Now, I'm pretty sure the decision had already been made before that conversation, but I didn't know it at the time. All I remember when walking out of the room, is that I had just chosen between living with my mom or my dad. As soon as I saw them, I burst into tears.

Those were tough days. Mom worked a lot to make ends meet. I remember her working three different jobs at one point–one in a factory and two serving tables. As a kindergartener, I walked to school in the morning and then to my aunt's house in the afternoon. The routine included an afternoon nap and then play time with my cousins. Mom would pick me up when it was getting dark outside. Sometimes, we would stay for dinner which for the most part was a treat. But, there were times when my aunt would serve harvard beets. Most of my family loved harvard beets; not me. I still get a shiver when I think about eating them. Fortunately, my uncle worked for Wonder Bread. There was always a stack of bread on the table. Everyone thought I loved Wonder Bread as I would eat four or more slices in a sitting. Don't get me wrong, I liked Wonder Bread, but the only reason I had four or more slices is because that is how many it took to get the harvard beets down.

Later that year, mom met a new friend. He took mom on special outings some evenings and on weekends. After one of the outings, they came home with buckets of smelt. Smelt are slender fish not much more than a few inches in length. In early Spring, smelt could be caught in shallow waters with hand-held dipping nets. We called it *smelt dipping*. Mom and her friend had been quite successful in their dipping efforts. Too successful! We had several freezer bags filled with smelt. It seemed like we had smelt and mixed vegetables at every meal. We ate them pan fried, bones and all. It wasn't long before I developed a dislike for that meal. In fact, I do not recall having eaten smelt since then although I have warmed up to mixed vegetables.

In addition to smelt dipping, mom's new friend introduced us to his family who lived just outside of town. While this friendship did not last very long, it was a significant point in time for mom and me. A Baptist church sat on the country road not too far from their house. We could see it when we turned down the lane where they lived, and we could see it on the hill across the fields from their house. It was the church that the family attended and with their encouragement it eventually became the place where mom and I began our spiritual journey.

It Was Hell!

A few weeks later, mom and I started attending that Baptist church just outside of town. It was named after one of the parks in the area, but the church's location was nowhere near the park. In fact, back then the church was surrounded by fields and the closest neighbors were a golf course, county roads facility, the local land fill, a cemetery, and the State prison. The location meant very little to me as I was quite proud of our church. It is where mom professed faith in Christ. And, where her spiritual journey took off. She quickly engaged in a ladies' Bible study, singing in the choir, participating in Awana, and taking on bus captain duties for one of the church's Sunday morning routes that picked up kids from the community for Sunday School. That meant I was also actively involved in these ministries playing quietly when the ladies came to the house for Bible study, rolling around and under the pews (sometimes falling to sleep) during choir practice, and getting up Sunday mornings while it was still dark outside for bus captain duties. While some of the ministry-related activities were less enjoyable than others for me, this was the beginning of my spiritual awakening as well.

The kids' ministry was likely normal compared to other churches in the area, but for me it was awesome! We had the best stories! Sang the coolest songs! Played the craziest games! We even got to meet celebrities like the real live Lurch from the Addams Family TV show! Pastor Russ was usually at the center of most of the fun including Lurch's visit. But, it wasn't only about fun. Pastor Russ would sometimes come visit at the house to toss the ball around and chat. He occasionally commented in the junior church lesson on how different ones of us were growing in our faith. Mike was one of his favorite guys in our group to call on when it was time to pray. Man could Mike pray! He knew all the right words to say and even got them in the right order as he prayed. I wanted to be like Mike.

One Sunday morning, Pastor Russ chose a topic for the junior church message that changed everything. It was hell! Literally, hell as in the place of fire and brimstone. Now, I had heard about hell before this message. It was a BAPTIST Church. I'm quite sure I knew every verse of *Just As I Am* by that point in my life and that song has a lot of verses. But this time, Pastor Russ described hell in a way that really concerned me.

He started by saying, "Hell is a real place. Do you know what it is like?"

We all said, "No."

"Well, hell is a place with fire. It is like turning all the burners on the kitchen stove and then jumping up on the burners." He said.

I thought, *that would be crazy! Who would do such a thing?* He went on to explain that the fires in hell lasted forever and that it was a horrible place of punishment for people who sinned against God. But God so loved the world that He gave His only begotten Son.

It is interesting how certain things come back to mind. I do recall a particular incident involving the burners of a kitchen stove. In fairness, it was my first experience with an electric stove. Mom took care to show me how it worked. She turned the knob on for one of the burners and said, "This is the heating element. Look at how it turns red hot when we turn the burner knobs on."

I had no clue what a heating element was, but I could clearly see that it turned red and I could certainly feel the heat emanating from it when the knob was turned on. As she turned the knob off and the redness went away, mom said, "Now listen. Even when the heating element isn't red anymore, it's still hot. Don't touch it!"

What possess a parent to say such things is a mystery to me because that clearly means *touch it* to a child. What was I to do? Of course, it had to be touched! It is entirely possible that what happened next had a profound affect in causing Pastor Russ' message on hell to resonate with me. Additionally, the Holy Spirit was working in me at that very moment helping me recognize that I was a sinner who needed to be saved and those wonderful words, "God so loved...", were finally beginning to make sense.

After church that morning, I told mom about the things Pastor Russ shared with us in the morning lesson. She asked me if I wanted to be sure that I would go to heaven and not hell. I was certain that I did not want to go to hell! In that moment, we both knelt by the hassock in the living room. With mom's leading, I prayed that Jesus would come into my heart and forgive me of my sin.

With Every Head Bowed

I didn't understand all the implications of salvation that day, but it is definitely the moment when I first acknowledged my sin and need for Jesus to save me. So, from my perspective, I was saved. To make things official though, it was understood that the next time I was in big people's church that I would need to walk down the aisle to the front of the church when everyone was singing *Just As I Am*. Walking the aisle was a common practice in our church. I rarely remember a service ending without us singing the song and seeing someone go to the front of the church. My heart was pounding as the service ended. You could tell the service was coming to a close because the music began playing and the Pastor had us all bow our heads and close our eyes. I often sneaked a peak. That is how I knew you were supposed to walk down the aisle during the song. "With every head bowed and every eye closed," I left my mom's side and walked down to the front of the church. Pastor Russ was waiting there at the front for me as was Mr. Stevens, Pastor Russ' dad and a deacon in the church. Mr. Stevens and I knelt and prayed together much like my mom and I had done the previous Sunday afternoon. When we were done praying, I was given the opportunity to tell everyone that I had accepted Jesus as my Savior. This was my first public profession of faith.

It didn't take me long to get the second profession of faith under my belt. The very next day I went to my first-grade teacher and said, "I got saved!"

With a concerned look on her face, she asked, "Were you in an accident? Was anyone hurt?"

"No! No! Nothing like that! I asked Jesus to come into my heart and He saved me from my sins." It was still okay to talk about God with your public-school teachers back then. I'm not sure if she was a Christian or not, but she seemed to know John 3:16 when I shared how God so loved the world. At any rate, my mom certainly had an opportunity to explain things more thoroughly at the next parent-teacher conference.

After telling my teacher, it was time to tell others in my family. I didn't have any siblings at this point, but I had cousins who were just a little younger than me. We spent a lot of time together in those days. One afternoon, we kids were out playing on the swing set. It was the typical back yard swing set with a glider and slide. While sitting on top of the slide, I started telling my cousins what I had learned in church about hell and the importance of asking Jesus to come into your heart. I remember praying out loud the prayer I prayed so that they could pray it too. I'm not sure if my attempt at witnessing made sense or not. All I knew was that I wanted my cousins to be in heaven with me and not in hell.

Baptism and Bus Rides

Making a public profession of faith and witnessing were important aspects of the Christian life that we learned in church. Another important aspect was a public demonstration of our faith through baptism. I had very little understanding regarding its significance, but I had seen several baptisms prior to my own. It was common for those who walked the aisle and professed faith in Christ to be baptized at the next baptismal service which usually took place in the Sunday evening service once a month. As it would happen, the Sunday after I walked the aisle was baptismal Sunday. So, that morning, I did not join my classmates in Sunday school. Instead, I joined a small group of mostly adults to receive instructions about being baptized. I was fortunate to be sitting next to a very sweet lady who helped me fill out the form and answer my questions. That evening, all of us that were in that morning class met with the pastor in the rooms behind the platform. Up till that point, I had only seen the baptismal from the auditorium. It was positioned front and center above and behind the choir loft. Soon it was my turn to step into the water. The

Pastor asked me some questions about how I accepted Jesus as my Savior and he baptized me. Water was no big deal to me because my Papa had taught me how to swim. When I came out of the water, I did what you are supposed to do after being dunked in water. I shook it out of my face and hair. Needless to say, some of the choir members got re-baptized that night.

I have many fond memories of those early days at church. One of the programs that took quite a bit of time, was the bus ministry. The bus ministry was a big deal and its success was largely due to the work of bus captains like my mom who faithfully visited the kids on the route each Saturday reminding them that the bus would be by the next morning to pick them up for Sunday school. It was also an opportunity for the bus captains to visit with the parents and do some door to door knocking to invite others to come along. I didn't always appreciate how faithful mom was with her route because I had to go along and some Saturdays it felt like we were never going to be done.

Undeterred by my occasional complaints, she would stop at each house on the route visiting with kids, handing out information packets to families, and offering treats on special occasions. After a while, I was familiar with the regular riders and enjoyed seeing everyone on Sunday when we picked them up. It's hard to imagine parents today being excited by a church bus showing up in front of their home Sunday morning and beep-beeping the horn, but that is what we did every Sunday morning. Most everyone on our route was friendly and easy to get along with. However, there was one exception. For no obvious reason, this one older kid we picked up always seemed out of sorts and generally difficult to get along with. One Sunday morning, the Pastor was driving our bus. Mom was the bus captain and, of course, sitting way up front where the bus captain was supposed to sit. I was always the first kid on the bus. So, I was way in the back—the very last seat which is the best seat on the bus for getting air time when you go over bumps in the road. We were getting close to the end of the route where the grumpy kid lived and all of us on the bus were grumbling about this kid. Before we stopped, the Pastor told us, "If you don't have anything nice to say, say nothing at all." Everyone was silent as the kid stepped on the bus, that is until I broke the silence. Being the literalist that I am and having a substantial number of seats between me and mom, I blurted out–NOTHING AT ALL! It was perfectly timed as the roar of laughter rose from the bus. Not even the Pastor was able to keep a straight face.

While I had pulled off one of the greatest comedic acts up to that point in my life, it was not without consequence. Mom was not amused. More importantly, God was not amused either. I had no idea what this boy had going on in his life that might have been contributing to the poor behavior. What I did know was that God so loved the world that He gave. The punishment from mom passed quickly, but the thought of how I treated this person, someone whom God loved, remains with me to this day.

God So Loved the World

It is hard to believe that more than four decades have passed since the beginning of my spiritual journey. There were some less than stellar moments like my bus ride humor at someone else's expense, but it was the beginning of a journey that I could not have imagined at the time. It all started with those well-known words, *For God so loved the world, that he gave his only begotten son, that whosoever believeth in him, should not perish, but have everlasting life.*

At first, I took those words very personally. God so loved me! He gave his Son to die for me! After that very personal understanding, I quickly applied the words to my family and others I knew. God so loved my dad, my grandparents, my cousins, and my teacher. I had to tell them! I had to be sure that they knew God so loved them and that they were saved! In family emergencies, I would ask–are they saved? Do they know God loves them? My mom was so supportive and very understanding of my concern. I'm not sure others in the family appreciated it as much. There was the time my grandma's dad, great grandpa Spencer, passed. Mom and I were with the family just before the memorial service. There was only one question on my mind and I made sure to ask the pastor. Was grandpa Spencer saved? I'm not sure how well the question was received by others, but I had to know. The pastor smiled and told me that grandpa was saved.

At some point in the years that followed, the words God so loved the world came into focus. The fullness of those words would cause me to consider God's bigger picture that reached beyond me, my family, and those in my immediate circle. His picture was the world. While I could not see it then, my spiritual journey would be a life in full-time ministry.

Chapter Two

How Firm A Foundation

Verse

By the grace God has given me,
I laid a foundation as an expert builder…
1 Corinthians 3:10

Introduction

"The wise man built his house on the rock." The parable from Matthew 7 has stuck with me from my days in Sunday school probably because when we sang the song our teacher dramatically exclaimed, "And the foolish man's house went splat!" Building a house on rock versus sand was all theoretical at the time, but I had a general understanding of the importance of laying a solid foundation as Paul described in 1 Corinthians 3:10. I was fortunate enough to have that theory made practical while in training to be a missionary with New Tribes Mission (NTM).

It was the Spring of 1989 just a few weeks after Sarah, our first daughter, had been born. Nancy and I were in the Pittsburgh, Pennsylvania (PA), area at one of NTM's training centers preparing for overseas ministry as church planters. That year NTM was preparing to relocate its missionary retirement center from Oviedo to Sanford, Florida (FL). NTM had acquired a 70-acre parcel of land that needed to be developed and homes built for the retirees. Several of us students were asked to travel down to FL and assist with the project. So, we packed up the mission vehicles with supplies and most of us guys headed off to FL for a few weeks to lend our aid.

When we arrived at the existing retirement center in Oviedo, it became our home for the next few weeks. Each morning we drove the 30-40 minutes to the worksite, a dusty field with a huge retention pond and one large shade tree where we gathered each day. The retention pond was important because after the shade tree it was the next most important meeting place on the worksite. All of us spent our breaks in the water cooling off. We weren't from FL and didn't realize there were two different types of water–swimming water which is in a swimming pool and alligator water which is everywhere else. We didn't much care at the time as it was hot and the water provided relief. I remember thinking as I looked around at everyone, *so this is why we only see the eyes and snout of gators in the water.* That was seriously the only part of your body that you wanted out of the water on a hot FL day. We were quite the sight. Fifty or more of us in the pond and the only things you could see were our hats and sun glasses.

Three of us were assigned to prepare the ground for eight houses to be built. I had worked on roofs before laying shingles, but I had never worked on preparing the ground for footers or slabs. The next couple weeks we dug trenches, tamped the ground, set up forms, put in rebar, and poured a lot of concrete. My fore arms still twitch when I think about running that tamper. At the end of our time in FL, we had the foundations in place for the eight houses. It was time to head back home as another crew would be coming in to carry on where we left off.

We were back in PA for about a week when the staff called us all to a special meeting in the chapel. They said, "We received another call from Sanford. We did such a fine job while we were there that they have invited us back."

"Really? How soon?" One of the guys replied.

"Right away. Pack your bags. We plan to pull out tomorrow morning." They said.

So, we packed our bags and the mission vehicles for the return trip to FL. I'll never forget the moment we set eyes on the worksite after being gone for ten days. The eight houses were completely framed, dried in, and ready for paint. I thought to myself, *you've got to be kidding me. All that work for three weeks to put some concrete in the ground. And in just ten days, the houses are built?*

In that moment, it became clear to me that not only was a firm foundation necessary, but that it took an incredible amount of work with very little to show for the effort. So, it is with laying a solid Biblical foundation. It requires time and effort. In the process, it is often hard to see the progress, but when done well the benefits are life changing.

The Children's Bible

The foundation in God's word began for me with *The Children's Bible* that mom gave me when we first started going to church. It was a book and record set produced by Peter Pan Records in the early 70's. There were two records which meant four sides of listening with 23 Bible stories that took me on a journey from the creation of the world to Pentecost. The stories were narrated with music and sound effects drawing attention to important details like who was speaking or when to turn the page.

"The creation of the world" the narrator would say with emphasis as he gave the title to the first story. Then with music playing in the background, he softly began telling the story of creation as though reading the words right from the Bible. "In the beginning, when God made Heaven and Earth...God said!" A thunderous clap sounded, and the powerful voice of God said, "Let there be light! And there was light," the narrator continued. "The light He called day and the darkness He called night. Then evening came, and morning came. This was the first day."

And so, the creation story would go with each day of creation. A thunderous clap of thunder would sound, God would speak, and whatever He said happened. It has likely been 40 years since I last listened to those stories. I can still hear the clap of thunder in my mind followed by the voice of God speaking everything into existence.

How I loved those stories! Fortunately, I was old enough to know how to set up and use the record player. (This was before the days of iTunes and YouTube.) Record players had speed settings, turn tables, arms that moved, and needles to be gently placed on the record so as to produce sound without causing damage to the needle or the record. I would play those records and follow along in the book for what seemed like hours. Over and over again, I would listen till I could pretty much recite the stories along with the narrator–sound effects and all. While I didn't realize it at the time, that repetitious listening was cementing details from God's Word into my mind and it was becoming a foundation that would influence the rest of my life.

Firmly Awana Stands

Wednesday night was Awana night at our church! We had a good-size Awana program. There were so many kids attending that we needed two full circles at game time. Mom was one of the leaders with the girl's group. That was back in the day when the boys and girls had separate clubs. The girls were the Chums and Guards and the boys were the Pals and Pioneers. This was also back in the day before Awana offered programs for the younger kids like me. It felt like torture being dropped off at the little kid's classroom on the second floor of the gymnasium. The classrooms were connected by a common balcony overlooking the gym. I could see all the other kids from the balcony as I went to my class. Throughout the night, we could hear everyone in the gym shouting and cheering as their teammates competed in the Awana games. They were having all the fun.

But the day finally came when I was old enough to join the Awana club. Wouldn't you know, that was the same year that Awana introduced a brand-new program for the younger kids. (But, I hold no bitter feelings about that whole season of life.) Not much really changed for the little kids. They still had to meet in the same old classroom on the second floor watching and listening to us big kids having fun downstairs in the gym.

We did have fun in Awana, but I quickly learned that there was more to the program than playing games. To be a member of the Pals club, our leaders gave us a pamphlet and said, "Boys, this is the Pals entrance test. Notice on the first page where it says Pals motto. You will need to memorize that and come say it to one of us leaders. That is the first section in your test that we will sign."

The other boy for Christ was the Pals motto. So, the first section was no big deal. The other sections included more things to memorize like the Pals key verse, the books of the Bible (all of them in order), and the Awana song which, by the way, was a really long song. To pass these sections, we would have to recite the content word perfect to our leader who would only give us a couple of helps. If we made more than three mistakes, he would make us start over. Once we finished all the sections in the pamphlet, we received our membership card which meant we got to move onto our first-year book with even more sections of stuff to memorize. I thought, *what on earth did I get myself into! I'm ready to go back to the little kids group!* But, there was no going back and besides that, the little kids now had entrance tests and books with sections to memorize too.

Mom would work with me in those early days to memorize my sections. I remember working on the books of the Bible together. We started with the New Testament. It seemed like work to get those 27 books down and then we moved on to the Old Testament which was another 39 books. We reviewed them repeatedly until I could recite them perfectly in order. This soon became a pattern with other sections and before long I was able to memorize the sections on my own.

Why do all that work? At the time, there were incentives on club night for quoting sections. We were divided up into teams and the teams that quoted the most sections for the night were given treats and prizes. The individual clubber who quoted the most sections received special recognition in front of the whole club. If we did that often enough, we could be recognized as clubber of the month and be given a special trophy. We also received achievement awards for completing major divisions in our books. Some of the awards were patches that were sown onto your club uniform, some were ribbons and pins that we also wore on your uniform, and for those of us who finished our books we received a nice plaque or trophy.

As much as I hate to admit it, I was totally into the awards and recognition. The ribbons and pins were cool looking and the trophies gave me a sense of accomplishment. I was the kind of kid who liked getting called up front when the awards were handed out.

Needless to say, my motivation was slightly off the mark. The awards were special, but the overall purpose in the Awana program was to build lives on the Word of God. Awana after all stood for *Approved Workmen Are Not Ashamed*. While I was in it for the awards, God was in it to firm up that foundation of His Word in my life. Yeah, I still have the trophies, ribbons, and pins. They serve as reminders of the incredible amount of effort that went into foundation work. More importantly, I had been immersed in God's Word through disciplined repetition and memorization. Many of the words and verses remain with me to this day.

Firmly Awana stands, led by the Lord's commands
Approved workmen are not ashamed,
Boys and girls for His service claim
Hail Awana! On the march for youth!
Hail Awana! Holding for the truth!
Building lives on the Word of God, Awana stands…

15

Dr. J Vernon McGee

It may be fair to say that I was above average when it came to Scripture memorization. The discipline and repetition involved came naturally to me and was something I enjoyed. There were many opportunities beyond Awana to engage in Scripture memory. We had a competitive church quiz team that I joined in high school. In preparation for a quiz meet, we would memorize multiple chapters of Scripture. Later in Bible school, we had Scripture memory class. It was the first class of the day. One semester was dedicated to memorizing the book of Philippians. Those who could memorize the book and recite it in one sitting would receive full credit without having to attend the class. That was totally on the must-do list considering it meant an extra hour of sleep for the whole semester.

Beyond the rigor of Scripture memory, I remember listening to radio programs like Sailor Sam, Ranger Bill, and Unshackled. These dramatized stories were fun to listen to and they always came with a life lesson based in Biblical principles. The Unshackled stories were based on real-life events. I met and worked with a gal whose life story was told on the show. It was a great way to see how the Bible made a difference in life.

One radio program that stands out in my memory above them all is Dr. J Vernon McGee's "Through the Bible program." It is possible that it stands out because of the opening and closing songs, or it might have been the distinct voice of Dr. McGee. It might have been his easy to understand teaching, or maybe it was simply the strategic time slot given by the radio station. The show was broadcast every morning and it just happened to be at the very time we were riding in the car to school.

I will confess that my earliest memories were not the greatest. When that song rang out, *How firm a foundation ye saints of the Lord,* I would roll my eyes and ask, "Mom, can we change the channel."

"No, we're going to hear what Dr. McGee has to say." She would answer.

In time, I stopped rolling my eyes and I started looking forward to hearing the program. I was beginning to hear and understand the Word of God in a new way. When Dr. McGee said "Friends" or "I mean to tell you", he was about to say something good. Dr. McGee's messages were a blessing.

It was evident through his teachings that he loved God's Word and that he wanted others to love it as well. Why? Because God's Word is the foundation of faith. It may have been purely happenstance, but I'm

16

guessing he picked the opening song for his program with purpose. *How firm a foundation, ye saints of the Lord, is laid for your faith in His excellent Word!*

God Spoke Their Language

I could not see as a boy how the Bible stories, Scripture memory, or radio messages were preparing me for the future. Like the long, hot days in FL preparing foundations to build houses, those activities as a boy were part of the foundation in God's Word that shaped my life. It wasn't clear at the time, but God's Word was the foundation that made all the difference in the world for me. And, having served in fulltime ministry most of my adult life, I have seen how God's Word makes all the difference in the world period.

Not many months ago, I was at a translation workshop with believers who had never before read God's Word in their own language. They had for decades been forced to be satisfied with reading or hearing God's Word in another language not their own. Could they understand truth from God's Word? Yes, it is true that they could understand it at least well enough to be saved. At the end of the first day of the workshop, the entire group gathered for an evening session to review the work that had been done earlier that day. As God's Word was read for the first time in their language, the emotion could not be contained. God spoke their language and it was as if His words had come alive. They were, in that moment experiencing what I had felt as a little boy listening to *The Children's Bible* over four decades ago. Finally, these dearly loved believers had access to God's Word in a language that spoke to them intimately. Finally, they had access to that solid foundation which is God's Word.

God is the master builder! He had a plan from the beginning for my life and it started with His Word as the foundation. I can think of no better way to serve Him then to engage in work that enables others to have the very same foundation.

Prayer

God, use me in laying the foundation of Your Word for others.

Chapter Three

Preacher Boy

Verse
*Preach the Word; be prepared in season and out of season; correct,
rebuke and encourage–with great patience and careful instruction.*
2 Timothy 4:2

Introduction

"Something has changed and not for the better. Even
Papa and Grandma have seen a difference in your behavior. We've
decided to enroll you in the local Christian school this year." These were
the words from my mom and step-dad the summer leading into my sev-
enth-grade year.

"Okay–do they have orchestra?" I asked.

"No, I'm sorry they don't."

*But, I'm first chair viola! Do you know how much work that took?
I'm not going to a school that doesn't have orchestra!* I thought to myself.
"Please don't do this! I'll do whatever you say! Just don't take me out of
the public school!" I pleaded.

"No! The decision has been made! You will be going to the
Christian school!"

They were right! Something had changed during sixth grade. That
was the year that all of us who graduated from the fifth grade moved from
Griswold Elementary to Frost Middle School. We went from being the
big kids at school to the little kids. Not only did we have to get used to
being the little kids again, we also had to get used to a completely different routine. We left the single classroom environment with the same

teacher all year to bouncing from one classroom to the next with a different teacher for each subject.

It was unsettling, and I found myself wanting to fit in with all the new kids, especially those in my homeroom class. The harder I tried the less I seemed to fit. So, I did what anyone in my situation would do, I started working on my comedy routine and began inserting commentary into the teacher's lessons. My timing was getting pretty good and generating a lot of laughs from my classmates, but the only thing I gained was a new seat in the seating chart–right next to the teacher in front of the whole class. I still don't understand how Ms. Karr thought moving me to the front of the room was going to help the situation. Maybe she thought it would shame me into better behavior. It only gave me a better platform to entertain.

Sadly, all my attempts to fit in failed. The only thing I successfully accomplished that year was completely ruining my reputation and losing my ability to witness for Christ. My feeble attempts at witnessing often ended with comments like, "You're not a Christian! Christians don't act like you!" They were right! I was not acting like a Christian; it was evident that I was way off course and missing out on God's plan for my life.

Preacher Boy Contest

It was my first day in a new school. We were all assembled in the gymnasium grouped by grade with our classmates, seven through twelve. It was the school's tradition to assemble all the students together on the first day to welcome the seventh graders to the combined junior-senior high school and to give everyone an inspiring message to start the new year. While welcoming the seventh graders, the Principal announced that we would each stand and introduce ourselves. I felt the nerves starting to kick in and I said to myself, "You are going to be okay, just say your name and quickly sit down." I was sitting at the far end of the first row and thought to myself at least I will get to see what everyone else does before it's my turn. Then the Principal said, "Let's start on the far end." So, I stood up and said, "My name is Timothy Forest Neu." The upperclassmen laughed! Apparently, I did not need to give my full name. Great! I just made a fool of myself in front of the entire student body.

Following the opening assembly, we were off to homeroom. We recited pledges to the flag, the Bible, and the Christian flag. This was a new experience for me as I had never heard pledges to the Bible or the Christian flag. After the pledges, Mrs. Howdeyshell, our homeroom teacher, led us in a short devotional and then shifted into our first class of the day. So far, everyone seemed friendly and we were off to a good start. Then it happened, Mrs. Howdeyshell made a mistake while writing on the chalk board. "Guess we need a new chalk board!" Someone said from across the room. "No, a new piece of chalk!" Came another. Being the astute person that I was, I chose to state the more obvious, "More like we need a new teacher!" No one laughed especially not Mrs. Howdyshell. In fact, she turned to me and said, "Tim, please go stand in the hallway. I will be with you shortly." Wow, kicked out of class on the first day, in the first five minutes. I was two for two in humiliating moments and the day was just getting started.

My guess is that Mrs. Howdyshell doesn't even recall the incident, but I remember it very well. Kicking me out of class was the best thing she could have done for me that day. It was the first time a teacher had called me out for misbehaving and then followed it up with a one-on-one conversation showing me what I did wrong and more importantly showing me how I could improve. Yes, I was embarrassed, but for some strange reason I felt like she truly wanted me to succeed. This was a turning point. Never again would I get kicked out of hers or any other class. I came to respect Mrs. Howdyshell and learned much through her faithful encouragement and coaching.

Part of that coaching included the daily devotional time that followed morning pledges. Each of us students were assigned days to lead devotions. I really enjoyed sharing and often filled in for my classmates when they forgot it was their turn. After class one day, Mrs. Howdyshell said that I should consider signing up for the preacher boy contest. The preacher boy contest was part of the annual fine arts festival that our school put on for the parents and faculty of the school. I was okay sharing in devotions with my friends, but speaking in front of all the parents and faculty was something entirely different.

I agreed to sign up for the contest and ended up being the only seventh grader in the competition. We were each given five minutes for our sermons which back then seemed like an eternity. This being my first time preaching, I went to Pastor Russ for advice. He suggested I go with John 3:16 and jotted down some talking points to get me started. I prepared three points because I had been told that is what makes for a good sermon. Then I practiced until it was perfect. The night arrived, and I sat in the front row of the church with the other preacher boys. Being the youngest, I went first. As I climbed the stairs to the platform, my heart was pounding so hard that I could hear it beating in my ears. When I turned to face the audience, I forgot everything that I had practiced. Fortunately, as I looked down at my notes, most of it came back and my five-minute sermon took all of three minutes to deliver.

It wasn't the greatest presentation, but it was good enough to earn second place in the contest. More importantly, it awakened a desire in me to preach and teach God's Word.

Child Evangelism Fellowship

Randy Manor was a fellow preacher boy and a good friend of mine who later encouraged me to date Nancy. But, long before either of us were dating, Randy introduced me to summer missions with Child Evangelism Fellowship (CEF). The summer before my freshman year in high school, we headed to Grand Rapids, MI, for CEF training. We spent two weeks on the campus of Grand Rapids School of the Bible and Music in preparation to be summer missionaries.

After settling into our rooms, we gathered in the assembly hall with a couple hundred other students to begin training. The opening session was led by Barth and Sally Middleton. We sang songs, listened to a Bible lesson, and heard a missionary story. The time flew by as the Middleton's made the Bible lesson and story time fun. In that time, they had demonstrated how a typical five-day club would be run. Following their presentation, we were divided into smaller classes to receive specific instructions in how to prepare for teaching five-day clubs.

This was my first time receiving formal instructions in preparing Bible lessons. In class, we were taught how to weave the gospel message into each lesson and how to include practical applications for those who were already saved. We learned how to effectively use our presentation booklets and other visual aids. After the first day, I was feeling pretty good with the format and thinking to myself, *this is going to be easy.*

It was time to practice in front of a live person. My first practice session was with one of our adult counselors. Memories of that preacher boy contest came rushing back as the nerves kicked in and everything I had practiced the night before disappeared from my mind. I taught what was supposed to be a twenty-minute lesson in less than ten minutes. My counselor smiled at me and said, "Well Tim, it looks like we need to work on a few things." It was not nearly so easy as the Middleton's or the instructors made it look. With the help of my counselor, I learned how to slow down and teach a complete Bible lesson. In time, I was having to work at keeping the lessons within the twenty-minute window.

By the end of our two weeks of training, I was a summer missionary with CEF. They had fully prepared me to teach five Bible lessons, share one missionary story with cliff hanger endings each day, and lead songs that supported the theme for the week. All the training and preparation resulted in an amazing summer teaching five-day clubs. I had the joy of sharing the gospel and seeing several kids accept Jesus as their personal Savior.

Pulpit Supply

"Be ready to preach, pray, die, or sing at any moment." That is the challenge I heard several times while in Bible school and missionary training. While they are not the exact words Paul wrote to Timothy when he said to be ready in season and out of season, the basic meaning is the same. Be ready at all times!

The exhortation to be ready was sound advice. One of my earliest experiences happened shortly after moving to Camdenton, Missouri (MO). Nancy and I had just entered NTM's language school to complete our training. Our first visit to one of the churches in the area started out as we would have expected. We were warmly welcomed as we walked into the sanctuary. The Sunday school teacher had us introduce ourselves and then went with the Bible study he prepared for the day. Following Sunday school, the Pastor introduced himself and just before heading up front to deliver the message he asked me to speak in the evening service. Before I had a chance to think, he was already up front introducing us to the congregation and announcing that I would be speaking in the evening service. That was only the beginning of preaching and teaching opportunities as I would soon be teaching adult Sunday school and occasionally sharing in the evening services.

There have been several situations over the years where I have had even less time to prepare. While I have been able to adjust and step in as requested, my preference has always been to have some lead. For the most part, the Lord has given me opportunities to speak with plenty of lead time. Such was the case with Union Gospel Church in Tipton, MI. After completing missionary training with NTM, Nancy and I took a staff position at NTM's Bible school in Jackson, MI. The director of the school had a speaking engagement that he was not going to be able to make. So, he asked me to fill in for him. It was a mission's conference at Union Gospel Church. I was honored that he would ask me and gladly accepted. That one conference turned into many repeat visits as the pastor of the church ended up following a ministry call to another church. I gladly filled in while the church looked for a new pastor.

Not all pulpit supply situations are created equal. I learned this lesson after accepting a speaking engagement in FL. By this time, our family had relocated to Sanford, FL, and were serving at NTM's corporate head-quarters. It was well known among the staff that I loved to teach and preach. A colleague approached me with a speaking opportunity at a local Church. This wasn't the first time I had taken a speaking engagement for this colleague. So, I just assumed it was a similar situation as those other times. I would prepare a general message with an emphasis in missions and tell as many NTM stories as time allowed. The schedule I received was straight forward; show up early, meet with the Pastor, deliver the message, and join the Church leaders for lunch after the service.

We started off by getting a couple of things right like showing up early and meeting the Pastor. From there it seemed to spiral downward as we were clearly not in synch with the culture of this Church. For example, there was a place of honor for Nancy and my girls to sit right next to the pastor's wife. Missed it! With small kids, Nancy chose to sit closer to the exit in case she needed to step out with the girls. I was supposed to join the Pastor and the Reverends (there were many) on the platform before the service. Missed it! I initially sat with my family. As the music played, everyone left their seats to come forward and place their offerings in the collection basket. Everyone! Missed that too! By the time I figured out what was happening the moment had passed.

When the Pastor gave the message before the message, he read from the big Bible on the podium and spoke at length without using notes. It was quite clear that I was unprepared for this situation because I had my own Bible in hand and I would need my notes to teach. It was noon when the Pastor introduced me. I thought I was just stepping into the pulpit when the service was supposed to be ending. My mind was racing. "How long do I speak? What am I going to say? I've prepared the wrong message!" As I stepped up to the pulpit, without hesitation I shared exactly what the Lord put on my heart and mind to say in that moment. It closely resembled the message I had prepared, but it was different. The congregation was actively involved, responding loudly in response to points that resonated, and answering questions I asked–even when I didn't expect an answer. I was feeling pretty good about the message as I returned to my seat. Evidently, I had not spoken long enough because the Pastor quickly returned to the pulpit to deliver an even more powerful, totally unrelated message.

We didn't end up having lunch with the Church leaders. They were polite in letting us know that plans had changed, but it was evident that we had failed to fit into the culture and lost an opportunity to be a greater blessing. That failure taught me that being ready in season and out of season is more involved than simply preparing to preach or teach a message from God's Word.

Teaching with Purpose

Fort Smith Boulevard Baptist Church (FSBBC) became our Church home for many years while we served at the corporate headquarters of NTM. Mark Benson, whom I'd known for years, took the senior pastor position before we joined. I graduated from high school with his daughter and served with him on staff at NTM's Bible school in Jackson, MI, prior to either of us moving to FL. It was a great joy reconnecting and serving with Mark in ministry at the Church.

FSBBC was a smaller Church during the time we were attending. Nancy and I had several responsibilities over the years. I did book-keeping, played guitar for a season, led choir, taught various Sunday school classes, participated in the Awana program, and filled in for Pastor Mark when he traveled. At some point along the way, I was ordained as an elder of the Church and joined Pastor Mark and another good friend of mine, Brian Zinnamosca, on the leadership team. We worked together to cast vision for the Church and coordinate the teaching efforts with purpose.

The Sunday school teaching slot for high school opened and I was asked to fill in for a few weeks. I agreed to fill in for a short time, but ultimately ended up continuing in the role for five years. It was a great group of young people who loved to study God's Word. We initially picked a book of the Bible to study and worked our way through it verse by verse. As the weeks passed, I began thinking about the high school program. We basically had four years to work with these young people. I asked myself, "What could we accomplish in four years?" A song from my past began ringing in my ears. *How firm a foundation ye saints of the Lord...* That's it! Let's take these young people cover to cover through the Bible in four years! I could think of no better way to prepare them for life after high school.

With Pastor Mark and Brian's blessing, we began developing and teaching a four-year program to the high school group. With great patience and careful instruction, we took the students through the Bible in four years. The first two years were dedicated to the Pentateuch and Old Testament history. That was followed with the life of Christ and Acts in year three and New Testament epistles in year four. It was an admittedly condensed overview, but by the end of the fourth year those who completed the course had a good working knowledge of the Bible as a whole. It is my understanding that they still use the four-year program with the high school class at FSBBC.

What Difference Does It Make?

I could not have imagined that a three-minute message from John 3:16 that I preached so many years ago would turn into a life of teaching and preaching. But, that is exactly what happened. Through preparation and training, I learned to preach the Word as Paul instructed his young protégé, Timothy. With practice and experience, filling in for pastors, I learned what Paul meant when he said to be prepared in season and out of season. As a teaching elder in a local church, I learned to teach the Word with great patience and purpose.

As I've grown in my understanding of Paul's instruction to preach the Word, I find myself giving a greater level of care in answering the question, "What difference does it make?" When Paul challenged Timothy to preach the Word in season and out, he indicated that God's Word is designed to make a difference in our lives. I firmly believe that God intended for His Word to grow us up in our relationship with Him. Indeed, knowing His Word and sharing it with others is essential both for me, and for those to whom I preach.

Prayer

Lord, continue teaching me Your Word showing me how it makes a difference.

Lord, continue using me to teach and preach Your Word so that it makes a difference in others.

Chapter Four

You're Too Young

Verse

Don't let anyone look down on you because you are young...
1 Timothy 4:12

Introduction

"You're too young!" I heard those words often.

"You're too young to ride the roller-coaster!"

"You're too young to date!"

"You're too young to get married!"

"You're too young to have kids...grandkids!"

Some of those statements were absolutely true. I was too young!

But at the time, I didn't see it that way. In fact, on many occasions, I didn't appreciate hearing those words at all. They irritated and frustrated me as did the people who said them. While I did my best to smile and take it, I did not always respond very well when someone told me I was too young. Sometimes I couldn't hold back a sarcastic, "Thanks! You're so kind for noticing!" Other times I would simply ignore it. That's why God gave us two ears–in one and out the other. Right?

In God's providence, He preserved words that Paul wrote to a young missionary named Timothy. "Don't let anyone look down on you because you are young..." It was easy for me to relate to this verse. I was Timothy after all and at the time I was young. I didn't realize it then, but these words would take on a deeper meaning as the years passed and the experiences increased.

Haunted Houses and Tilt-a-whirls

Some of my earliest memories of hearing the words, "You're too young," involve haunted houses and amusement park rides. With a few traumatic experiences, I learned that those words were at times true. I was indeed "too young"! I also learned that height requirements for certain rides, while extremely annoying to young adventurous boys, are there for a reason.

I remember one occasion when I failed to meet the height requirements to get on a ride at the county fair. It was the Tilt-a-whirl. Everyone riding the Tilt-a-whirl looked like they were having the best time ever. Whooping and hollering! Laughing and carrying on! The height requirement did not exactly prohibit shorter people from riding. There was the option of being accompanied by an adult. Naturally, I turned to my mom and asked, "Can we ride the Tilt-a-whirl? Please?"

"I don't think so. You're too young for that ride." She said.

"But the sign says younger riders can ride with an adult." I said.

"No. We're not riding the Tilt-a-whirl. You're too young."

The reality is that mom had said that phrase a time or two before. One might think I would have learned to listen to mom from previous encounters. Like the time she said, "You're too young to go into the haunted house by yourself." I totally ignored that warning and snuck in on my own. That decision I instantly regretted! Mom of course came to my rescue. But, I failed to remember that event and continued begging mom to take me on the Tilt-a-whirl. It would have been a lost cause except there was a more rational adult with us on that day. Yes, my uncle came to my aid or so I thought.

"Linda, I think we should let the boy have some fun. Let's take him on the ride." He said.

She agreed and the three of us made our way onto the ride. Oddly, things did not go at all like I imagined. The thrill of the ride quickly turned into sheer terror and the whooping and hollering I heard from others who had gone before me turned into screams of get me off this thing! Fortunately, the ride operator graciously stopped the ride early to let us off.

19 Year Olds

There are those haunted house and tilt-a-whirl moments in life where the words "you're too young" needed to be said and heeded. It is not a forever thing, but rather a season. That season passes quickly. Soon

28

thereafter is that season where you know that you are no longer "too young". You are ready to step onto that ride without an adult, but the adults in your life may not see it that way.

I remember this season of life all too well. As a high school student, there were two things that I was fairly certain were in my near future–getting married and going into fulltime ministry. Interestingly enough, I was dating a blond-haired, blue-eyed beauty who would one day become my wife. Of course, I was "too young" to be dating seriously. At least that was the common thought of those around me, but I was pretty sure she was the one for me. After 34 years of dating and 30 years of marriage, I think it is safe to say that I was right.

It was in those high school years that I felt the leading of the Lord to pursue full-time ministry. At the time, I had in mind to pursue the pastorate having been inspired by a couple of different pastors in my life. Pastor Gould was a gifted expositor who brought the Bible to life by teaching us the meanings of the text using Biblical languages and weaving in the culture of the day. Pastor Jones was amazingly compassionate, keenly aware of the needs of others, and genuinely caring—a true shepherd. Both men influenced me greatly as a high school student.

With an eye on marriage and ministry, the accepted or rather expected path forward was to enroll in a college, get a degree, and then get married. I was in total agreement with all those things except the order. For me, marriage was much higher on the priority list and something I unashamedly made known. It was no surprise to me in the least to hear the words, "You're too young," from my mom, then from my grandparents, and even from my Pastor. While ready for those words, I was not ready for the other words that followed. In addition to being "too young", one of my mentors and someone I highly regarded said, "19-year-olds can't possibly know the will of God for their life."

Could it be true? Is someone too young at age 19 to know God's will for his life?

It became a defining moment for me. I was faced with a decision of moving forward with what I felt in my heart was God's leading in my life or listen to the counsel of others that I had depended on through my formative years. In an effort to demonstrate that I valued the input of others, I chose a modified order to the expected path by attending my first year of Bible school single and then getting married. While still not the popular path among those around me, it was clear to me that God was leading in those decisions. I was moving from a place of dependence on others for knowing His will, to directly depending on Him, even if it meant others looked down on me.

Office Management

In my mid-20's, I experienced a shift in attitude towards the "You're too young" comments—a shift from irritation and frustration to "challenge accepted." *So, you think I'm too young, do you? We'll just see about that!*

The year was 1993. Nancy and I were living in Jackson, MI, serving as missionaries at New Tribes Bible Institute. My primary role was book-keeping, but I took on as many responsibilities as the leadership would give me. All of us on staff performed numerous duties from stripping and waxing floors in the summer to mentoring groups of students during the school year. I occasionally had the opportunity to share in chapels and even the privilege of teaching classes. Outside the daily duties, we lived life with the students. We were the same age as many of them and they became our closest friends.

One morning, early in the fall semester of '93, the Chairman of the school leadership committee came into my office and said, "Tim, we would like you to join us in the conference room. We have something important to discuss with you." It felt like I had been called into the prin-cipal's office. I wondered what we had done wrong. The chairman spoke first. "Tim, how do you like oranges?"

I thought to myself, *did he just ask me how I like oranges?* "I don't understand the question." I said.

"Let's get to the point." One of the other guys said.

"Tim, we received a call from the guys in Sanford. There's an opening at the Headquarters in the finance office. They need someone to move to FL and manage the finance office. They asked for you." It was a relief to hear that I wasn't in trouble and that I was being offered a management role at the Headquarters.

I accepted the offer and a new journey in ministry began. This part of the journey took me deeper into the financial side which was quite a bit different then what I had originally planned. It was a new focus, a new location, and a completely new team with very few people my age. The truth is that I was the youngest with the majority of team members being my parent's age and older.

I joined the team as their new leader which had to be as challenging for them as it was for me. While I felt up to the task, I clearly had a lot to learn. At least, that is how I was viewed by some on the team. No one ever said it, but I felt the, "Who is the young guy?" question in the nonverbal feedback. I did have a lot to learn about the systems and processes, but I had something they didn't have–a fresh perspective.

It was a "you're too young–challenge accepted" moment in life. Rather than assert my position and authority, I chose to sit with each person and methodically learn how to do everyone's job. Every step of the way, I documented the roles and reviewed the details of every procedure until we had a complete operation's manual. In the process, it quickly became evident that everyone had a specialty job and basically worked in isolation even though we were all in the same open office space. Because of the specialization, some would finish up their part of the daily tasks early in the day and leave. Others were required to work late into the evening.

Armed with a fairly complete understanding of the systems, processes, and a fresh perspective, this young guy did the unthinkable. I called the team together and said, "We are a team! As a team, we need to learn each other's jobs." Then I went on to explain that we needed to have overlap so that people could be gone without massive amounts of work piling up and so that everyone could end their day at the same time. The initial response was as you might expect. This young guy has lost his mind. The good news is that we had already gained confidence in each other as I had spent a great deal of time with each person learning their jobs. In that time, we weren't only learning processes and procedures. We were learning to live life together and grow in our genuine care for each other. With that level of care came a trust and together we forged a new path forward in unity instead of isolation.

Executive Leadership

Success in leadership often leads to more responsibility. I continued taking on more and more responsibilities, but at times questioned myself just like others had when they commented on my being "too young". This was a new season. One where I remember asking myself, "Am I too young?" It was more an internal questioning of my own readiness compared to the Lord's readiness to use me.

The question of readiness came sharply into focus one hot and humid summer afternoon in Camdenton, MO. Our family had made a trip to New Tribes Mission's language training center where we participated in an annual conference held for the organization's overseas staff members who were in the States. The conference was an opportunity for staff from all aspects of the ministry to gather for refreshment and to hear from the organization's leadership.

I was approached by the Executive Committee Chairman that hot and humid afternoon. He said, "Tim, the Executive Committee wants to meet with you to discuss something important." It wasn't the conference room in Jackson, MI, but nevertheless, it felt about the same. People didn't get asked to meet with the highest level of leadership unless it was serious. This time no one asked me a question about oranges or fruit of any kind. The Chairman got right to the point. "Tim, we would like you to consider joining the Executive Committee." I thought, *What? Join the executive committee?*

The Executive Committee was made up of men that had served in significant positions of leadership around the world. Many of them had years of experience trekking through the bush, working with indigenous peoples, planting churches, and were known by all for their great faith. I had not even been overseas at that point in my career with New Tribes Mission. Most of these guys were in their 60's. I was in my early 30's. My mind was shouting at me, "You're too young!" and I wondered if it might be right. But these men saw something that I wasn't seeing in myself and they extended the invitation to join them in leadership.

With much prayer and Godly counsel from my closest friends, I accepted the invitation to join the executive committee. I was given responsibility for all the financial aspects of the organization and functioned as the CFO. As the CFO, I had responsibility for corporate accounting, financial reporting, internal and external audit, investments, employee benefits, risk management, and tax. This assignment was not done completely in a vacuum. I had completed an MBA with an emphasis in executive leadership prior to the invitation to join the executive leadership team. In addition, I had been working with a great group of financially skilled guys who continued serving in their respective roles through my time as CFO.

Despite my initial feelings of inadequacy and youthfulness, the Lord enabled us to make some significant enhancements in the areas of finance. Very early in my time as CFO, we implemented the first ever corporate budget. This enhancement was an area that I had been working on for some time prior to my appointment to the executive committee. The leadership role made it much easier to see the implementation through to completion. Along with budgeting, we enhanced the area of investments by updating the investment policy statement from a single to multipage document incorporating prudent investor standards. This enabled us to expand the organization's ability to invest and generate additional revenues in support of the operations. We also enhanced the employee self-funded benefits program by incorporating stop loss coverages to limit the exposer of the pool of funds to catastrophic losses. It turned out that I had the skills needed to be the CFO and God showed me that I wasn't too young after all.

Forever changed

Amazingly, I still hear those magic words, "you're too young", But it's okay. It brings a smile to my face as it clearly beats other words that could now be spoken like "you're too old" which will usher in an entirely different season of life.

It would seem as though I have been afforded a great opportunity to grow deeper in my understanding of the thought that Paul conveyed to Timothy when he said, "Don't let anyone look down on you because you are young". Each season of life brought a slightly different understanding of Paul's words. There were times I needed to listen and heed the exhortation of others, times I needed to stand on decisions that made no sense to those around me, and times to step out in faith when I considered myself to be too young.

There is yet another aspect of Paul's words that came into focus on a cold fall afternoon in the foothills of the Nepali Himalayas. I was attending a Bible translation workshop where a small group of believers had gathered to translate the New Testament into their language. Several special moments took place at that workshop and forever changed my view of Bible Translation. One of those moments happened towards the end of the event when the youngest member of the translation team, a teenage girl, translated Paul's first letter to Timothy. She paused as tears filled her eyes. When asked if she was okay, her response was that the passage she just translated was written to her–"don't let anyone look down on you because you are young."

For me, "Don't let anyone look down on you because you are young" has now become, "Don't look down on others because they are young."

Prayer

Lord remind me that it was You working in and through me when I was "too young".

Lord remind me that You are working in and through others–even those who are "too young".

Chapter Five

In Sickness and Health

Verse

Husbands, love your wives, just as Christ loved the church…
Ephesians 5:25

Introduction

"She's the one! Nancy is the one that I am going to marry!" I told my classmates one morning in chemistry class.

"How can you possibly know that for sure?" asked one of the upperclassmen in the room.

My response was simple: "I love her! That's how I know!"

Being in love as a high school student was considered cute, but not many expected it to last. After all, what could high school students possibly know about love. Well, this high schooler felt like he had a pretty good handle on the subject. I read the books, listened to the lessons in church and at school, and I studied up on what it truly meant to love someone like Christ loved the church. Love was more than feelings. It was about commitment and sacrifice. In theory, I understood what it all meant. I even remember saying the very words that Peter said to Jesus, "I'll die for you." That is, after all, the model that Jesus gave when He died on the cross in our place. His act was the ultimate expression of love. Wasn't it?

This year, Nancy and I celebrated our 30th wedding anniversary. There has not once been a moment when I have been called upon to die for her–physically. Instead, there have been countless opportunities to live a life of love with her. In those moments, I began learning what commitment and sacrificial love really meant. I say *began* because it would seem as though there is more to learn about living love with every day that passes.

September 29th

It was the '82-83 school year, and the class was Geography. For all practical purposes it seemed like every year before, but something was about to change. Mid-year, we had a new student join the class. Her name was Nancy Raetz. She had beautiful blue eyes and an amazing smile. I would later find out that her impression of me was that I was the boy in class with his own box of facial tissue who quite often blew his nose. It was true, I had terrible allergies at certain times of the year. I'm just thankful that her first impression of me wasn't her last.

About mid-semester, the school held its annual junior-senior banquet. This would have been the equivalent of the prom at other schools. The primary difference was that we didn't dance at least not at the event. It was called the junior-senior banquet because the junior class was responsible for putting on the event in honor of the seniors which included decorations, dinner menu, invitations, and the evening program. Sophomores were automatically invited and strongly encouraged to attend as they would be the hosts of the banquet the following year. Freshmen were not invited. There was an unspoken waiver for freshmen that everyone understood though and that was they could attend if accompanied by an upperclassman.

I was one of those freshmen not invited to the banquet until one of my buddies from the sophomore class asked me for a favor. He said, "Tim, I asked my girl-friend to the banquet. She said yes. But I need to find her best friend a date. How about it? Would you ask her friend to the banquet?"

"Me? Ask an upperclassman to the banquet? Absolutely! Who?" I asked.

"Nancy Raetz." He said.

"The new girl? From geography class? The one with the blue eyes and amazing smile? Nancy Raetz?"

"Yes, to all that!" He said as he assured me that she would indeed go with me to the banquet. So, I worked up the courage and asked her. She said she needed to ask her parents for permission and would get back with me the next day.

The rest of that day I was on pins and needles wondering if she would be able to go with me. I couldn't wait to get home to tell my mom and step-dad the great news. Well, I was in for a rude awakening! "You're all smiles tonight. Have a good day at school?" They asked.

"Good? It was a great day!" I exclaimed. "I asked an upperclassman to the upcoming banquet."

"The junior-senior banquet?" They asked.

"Yeah, that one." I said.

"Well, you'll have to un-ask her because you're not going." They obviously hadn't heard about the waiver—the one that clearly allowed freshmen to attend the banquet when accompanied by an upperclassman. I explained it to them in a most respectful way, but they didn't budge. Their word was final, and I wasn't going to the banquet.

Well, my parent's decision left me in a rather precarious situation. I had already asked Nancy to go with me to the banquet. My next conversation with her was one of the most embarrassing moments in my life. She had that amazing smile on her face and I knew before she spoke a word that her parents had given her permission. I swallowed hard and told her that I would not be able to take her to the banquet. It was a painful experience, but I made sure moving forward to check with my folks before asking someone out to a school banquet.

My buddy ended up taking both his girlfriend and Nancy to the banquet while I stayed home. It worked out all right though because that wasn't the only banquet in the school year. A few months later, there would be the homecoming banquet and that time I had permission in advance. On September 29, 1983, I asked Nancy to go with me to the homecoming banquet and we have been dating ever since.

Love, Honor, and Cherish

The day had finally arrived! It was a beautiful MI day in June 1987. Family and friends from out of town had mostly arrived by the morning of the 13th. Mom made my favorite breakfast, and everyone was getting ready to head over to the church. I was, of course, anxious to get on with the day. Nancy and I had been dating for four years which from my perspective was long enough.

I arrived at the church slightly ahead of schedule. This was in keeping with my driving instructor's number one rule regarding timeliness. I can still hear Mr. Furnace's words ringing in my ears as he explained his rules, "To be on time is to be late! To be early is to be on time!"

The planning was complete, decorations were in place, our guests had arrived, and the bridal party was ready. It was time to begin a new chapter in our lives as husband and wife. The groomsmen and I stepped into place as the music began. Each of the bridesmaids made their way to the front just as they had practiced the night before. Then Nancy and her dad stepped into the doorway at the back of the church. She was so beautiful in her wedding dress, that I couldn't take my eyes off her. After presenting Nancy to me, her dad took his place on the platform to marry us. Looking back, I do not know how he managed to make it through the service without even a crack in his voice. (Nancy and I would later be blessed with two daughters who are now both married. I managed to walk Sarah, our oldest, to the front of the church, but when I turned to give her one last hug as my unmarried daughter I totally lost it and the tears flowed. It would have been nearly impossible to say a word let along speak in front of a group.)

Our ceremony was very traditional with singing, a brief message, reciting vows, exchanging rings, unity candle, and the all-important wedding kiss, followed by the proclamation of us as husband and wife. After the message, we recited our vows to love, honor, cherish, for better or worse, richer or poorer, in sickness and in health, as long as we both shall live. We had carefully considered these words and practiced saying them to each other many times prior. They represented a deep commitment and a willingness to sacrifice. When we said those words in front of our family and friends that day, we were ready! While we loved each other enough to say the words, we didn't really know how much deeper our love would grow as we lived them.

Daughters

"It's a girl!" Came the words from the other room; only it wasn't the birthing room and it wasn't the voice of the doctor. I knew this because I was in the birthing room looking right at the doctor who was helping Nancy deliver our first child. Sarah had let out her first cry before anyone could possibly know that she was a girl. But, from that precious little cry, my step dad who was in the room next door knew it was a girl and had proudly proclaimed it. She was so tiny and had the cutest little cry. That little cry would eventually become much louder and not quite as cute.

It might seem strange to some, but I had always wanted a daughter. Nancy and I had lived in married couples' housing while in Bible school. Our neighbors had the sweetest little girl. Every night, she would run down the hallway with all the energy and enthusiasm she could muster to greet her daddy when he came home from work. That was something

I wanted to experience as a dad. So, I asked the Lord to give us a girl. He heard my prayer and actually gave us two. Stephanie was born exactly two years later, a birthday gift for her big sister.

I was there by Nancy's side for the birth of both our girls. (Here is a word of wisdom to the young guys who think they're tough. Do not wear a ring, especially a larger one like a class ring while holding that hand of a spouse who is in the middle of birthing a child. The transference of pain leaves a lasting impression on the adjacent fingers.) Nancy demonstrated the most amazing grip strength while enduring that pain. There wasn't much I could do to comfort or bring relief from the pain, but soon after the girls were born one would hardly know she went through all that pain. It's the most amazing experience in life to witness— that something so painful produces so much love. My admiration and love for my wife jumped to a whole new level.

The girls brought all the joy I had imagined and so much more. It was fun being superman for a season. We had tickle wars, did tumbling exercises, and played indoor soccer using doorways and furniture as goals. Every so often, mommy would join in to help the girls gang tackle daddy. I of course, let them win from time to time.

It was a busy season of life for us as a family. I was on staff at New Tribes Bible Institute in my home town of Jackson, MI. We were active in our church, attending services, teaching youth, and singing in the choir. The Bible school had tons of activities for the staff and students. I was majorly involved in the sporting events, playing soccer and basketball a couple of nights a week. There were also the occasional visits to the tennis courts and golf courses. Looking back, it was a crazy schedule, but I was having fun. It seemed to work at first, but being out of the house as often as I was, soon, had to stop. Life was changing!

Practicing Medicine

Nancy was not herself. She was fatigued all the time and barely able to keep up with the basic things for the girls. I would come home from the office and the house looked like a tornado hit it. Actually, two tornadoes had hit and their names were Sarah and Stephanie. Nancy would be lying on the couch with the unfolded laundry still in the basket. This may sound normal to some, but it was clearly not normal for us. Something was seriously wrong!

The primary care doctor said this was life. We had two small kids and we lived at a Bible school with a bunch of other people sharing colds and flu bugs. Fatigue should be expected. What did we know? We just assumed the doctor was right and that this was the new normal, but it was taking a serious toll on our relationship. Then one morning as we were waking up, Nancy mentioned to me that her heart felt like it was racing. I checked her pulse and it was 130!

"Did you have a bad dream?" I asked.

"No," she said. "I've been lying here awake feeling too tired to get up."

It's no wonder she was too tired. Who has a resting heart rate of 130? Someone with Graves' disease.

We would later find out that Nancy had an autoimmune condition that caused her body to attack certain organs in her endocrine system. The first was her thyroid and next was her pancreas. Her thyroid went hyperactive which caused unusually high resting heart rate and the pancreas just all of the sudden quit producing insulin.

With the thyroid episode, one might think that we would have recognized the signs of yet another physical condition. Years had passed since the thyroid condition and at age 31 we had no reason to consider the possibility of Nancy becoming a type 1 diabetic. Looking back, the signs were obvious. She was constantly thirsty, ate more food at meals than me, and was losing weight fast. In just a few short weeks, Nancy dropped to 90 pounds. I thought we were going to lose her. Fortunately, our doctor recognized what was happening and quickly got her on the needed insulin therapy.

The autoimmune condition created some scary moments, but those issues were quickly diagnosed and while life changed it was easy enough to manage. During the years in between the thyroid and pancreas episodes, Nancy went through a season of pain that baffled the doctors. It was seven long years with thirty different doctors suggesting multiple medications and therapies. Hence the phrase, *practicing medicine*. At its absolute worst point, Nancy would be down in bed for weeks at a time unable to function. I remember holding her as she trembled uncontrollably from the pain. It was the most helpless feeling I have every experienced—seeing her in so much pain and knowing there was nothing I could do. To make matters worse, there was nothing the doctors could do either, or so it seemed.

Close friends of ours, Scott and Deb Ross, suggested we visit the urology clinic at the University of Washington in Seattle. Why Seattle? As it happened, Scott's sister-in-law was a nurse in the urology clinic and the doctor was well known for working with patients who were suffering with pain like Nancy was experiencing. People from all over the world were flying into Seattle to see this doctor.

As supported missionaries based in the US, we didn't have much income much less savings to take a trip to WA. Some other friends of ours heard about the possibility of us getting help in WA and they gave us frequent flyer miles so that we could make the trip. We were on our way to Seattle. The first couple of days were spent in consultations and running tests. Despite the pain Nancy was experiencing at the time, I was able to drive her around the area to see some of the local scenery while we waited for the results. Seattle is surrounded by some spectacular mountain views. The most breath-taking for me was Mt. Rainier. It was only visible from the city for a couple of the days we were there, but it was amazing.

Soon the results were in and the doctor had news for us. It was the good news/bad news discussion. The bad news was that Nancy was suffering with interstitial cystitis (IC) a condition that she would live with the rest of her life. Hearing this was quite a blow. We had been hoping for a cure. But praise God there was some good news. The doctor went on to say that he had actually had success in treating IC symptoms. He then prescribed medications for managing the pain.

Finally, a diagnosis! Finally, some relief!

I Would Do It All Again!

The IC has proven to be exactly what the doctor in Washington said, a lifelong event. Nancy has had seasons of relief from the pain, but it raises its ugly head periodically reminding us that modern medicine, as wonderful as it is, cannot solve all health issues. In the seasons of pain, I have seen Nancy grow deeper in her love for the Lord. Some days even now are tough, but by God's grace she has found peace in the pain and strength to press on. It reminds me of the days that our girls arrived. All that pain and yet the depth of love it produced.

Sadly, I must admit that I have not always been the most understanding or the most gracious. I didn't really understand what it would take to love in sickness and in health when I said those words over 30 years ago. It never crossed my mind when we were standing there in front of our family and friends that sickness and pain would be such a big part of our lives.

Would I have said those words had I known? Would I commit to doing it all over again? Without a doubt–absolutely! Yes! How else would I have learned how to love this deeply? How else would I have learned how to love like Christ?

Prayer

Lord, thank you for teaching me how to love so deeply through my wife.

Lord, give me wisdom and grace to keep learning to love like you love as we journey on together.

Chapter Six

Obey All Things

Verse

*Therefore, go and make disciples of all nations, baptizing them in the
name of the Father and of the Son and of the Holy Spirit, and teaching
them to obey everything I have commanded you …*
Matthew 28:19-20

Introduction

By the time I was a student in high school, my family had changed
churches. Cascades Baptist Church was just a few blocks from our house.
Even though we now live several States south of Michigan, I still refer to
it as my home church. Tony Gould was our pastor. While it was before the
days of Power Point, Pastor Gould used overheads and slide projectors to
add visual aids as he taught. I remember very early in my time at Cascades
wanting to be a pastor someday, and to teach just like Pastor Gould.

It wasn't a secret. Whenever someone asked what I was going to
do after high school, I would say, "I'm going to Bible school and then
become a pastor." Often, folks would respond by suggesting which school
would be the best for preparing me for pastoral ministries, usually the one
they attended.

I had already started dating Nancy by the time I was a sophomore
in high school. She was the daughter of missionaries who had recently
returned from five years of ministry in Indonesia. Our dates were typically
spent in the company of our friends or parents as we were not allowed
to be out alone. One of our favorite activities was playing Rook while

eating nachos and cheese with Nancy's mom and dad. I loved playing card games, eating snacks, and most importantly spending time with Nancy.

"What are you going to do after high school?" Nancy's dad asked one night.

I gave my normal response, "I'm going to Bible school and then becoming a pastor."

Then he asked the most unusual question in response, "Have you ever considered becoming a missionary?"

I don't remember where the conversation went from there, but I was pretty sure at that point in time that I was meant to be a pastor.

10ᵗʰ Grade Bible Class

Bible class was required every year at the Christian school. We often had a pastor from one of the local churches teach us Bible. For 10th grade, Pastor Khuns from Lansing Avenue Baptist Church taught our class. He was a no-nonsense teacher who commanded respect in the classroom; for himself, for each other, and most importantly for the Word of God. His approach to managing the classroom made an impression on me as I would later employ a similar approach when teaching Bible to high school students.

Pastor Khuns taught the book of Romans the first semester and missions the second semester. Romans class was a typical book study that took us chapter by chapter through Paul's letter to the Romans. Missions on the other hand was a topical study on the Great Commission passages. The first passage he chose was Matthew 28:18-20. It may not have been the first time I had heard or read these verses, but I clearly remember it as the first time I was confronted with Jesus' command to "make disciples of all nations."

What is the Lord trying to say? My girlfriend is a missionary kid who is gung ho for missions. Her mom and dad have encouraged me to consider being a missionary. The Scriptures seem to be pointing to a broader ministry focus–"all nations". Some of my friends were considering foreign missions. Am I supposed to be a missionary?

To determine what the Lord was really saying to me, I started looking into what it meant to be a missionary. I listened more intently to missionaries when they came to our church and visited with them after their presentations. NTM had a Bible school in town where Nancy's mom and dad served on staff. The school had conferences and offered night courses that I frequented. Before long, I was sensing that God wanted me to be a missionary.

By the time I was a senior in high school, I had a different answer to the question, "What are you going to do after high school?"

"I'm going to Bible school and then becoming a missionary."

Feeling Homesick

It was a new adventure. I had just graduated from high school, Nancy and I were engaged, and we were on our way to Bible school. Our destination was 915 N Hartwell Ave. in Waukesha, Wisconsin (WI), the New Tribes Bible Institute. It was not a difficult journey. We simply got on I-94 just outside Jackson and headed West for six hours driving through Chicago and Milwaukee until we saw the exit sign for Waukesha.

As we turned down Hartwell Ave, we could see the main building at the top of a hill. It was an older structure that once served as a community hospital. NTM purchased it years before and converted it into the school that we would call home for the next two years. We drove up the hill to the main entrance of the school and went inside to complete our final registration for the semester. The receptionist called our room proctors who came down to give us a quick tour of the campus and show us our rooms.

The first couple of days were a little overwhelming. I remember feeling homesick, but wasn't about to say anything to Nancy. After all, we were adults engaged to be married.

The newness quickly faded and the busyness of campus life began. We both signed up for the maximum number of classes offered each semester, wanting to seize the opportunity to take in as much Bible teaching as we could in those two years. Some of our classes were a single book of the Bible like Romans and Ephesians while other classes were groups of books like Pentateuch and Old Testament History.

We kept busy while in Bible school. There was plenty to do on campus with intermural sports, work detail, and spending time with our friends. I was on one of the basketball teams with weekly games and a tournament towards the end of the semester. Occasionally I also played a soccer game and some tennis. I wasn't great at tennis, but I became good friends with one of our instructors who was kind enough to invite me to play a match from time to time. We would often discuss the key points covered in class. It gave me insights into how he viewed the passages we were studying that I hadn't picked up in the short time we were given in class.

Off campus, we were active in the local church, helping with Awana and teaching a weekly Bible study. And, we worked! The school had a policy regarding employment. Students were limited to twenty-five hours of work a week. It seemed odd to have such a policy, but we signed statements saying we understood and would abide by the rules. All the rules! There were others that we didn't much like, but this one rule in particular had the potential of limiting our ability to earn enough funds to keep current on our school bill. We met with the dean of students and asked, "How strong is the school on the employment rule?"

"Well, it depends. What did you have in mind?" He responded.

"We are concerned that the hours limitation for employment may make it difficult to stay current with our school bill." We said.

"What kind of grades do you normally get?" He asked.

"We usually get A's." We replied.

"Okay. This is what we will do. If you can maintain a 3.0 or higher, you can ignore the 25-hour limitation for employment." He said.

We were both over-achievers and quite competitive, especially with each other, when it came to grades. We ended up working close to fulltime hours through Bible school. It was a crazy schedule, but we managed to survive the busyness with our bills paid and money in the bank to cover our next level of training with NTM.

I thoroughly enjoyed taking in the teaching from God's Word. Then there was homiletics, a class that many dreaded because it involved public speaking. For me, it was the icing on the cake because I loved teaching God's Word. I remember one of the first assignments. The only instructions given–preach a twenty-minute missionary challenge! That's it! The passage that made the most sense to me for this assignment was Matthew 28:18-20. I went to the instructor after class to ask, "Do you think this passage will be used by other students? Should I choose another passage?" He said, "You should go with the passage God puts on your heart and mind to preach regardless of what the other students choose." I did exactly that!

Matthew 28:18-20 was instrumental in challenging me into missions. It meant even more after I studied it for myself and preached that message for homiletics. Amazingly, I was the only student in class who spoke from that or the other *Great Commission* passages.

Boot Camp

Nancy and I were married the summer between our first and second year of Bible school. So, we finished our time at Bible school as a young married couple ready to conquer the world of missions. After graduation, we packed up our few belongings and headed to Rochester, PA, for our next phase of training with NTM. That year would be a practical application of the knowledge we acquired in Bible school.

The missions training course back in those days was nicknamed Boot Camp, likely a carryover from the early days of training that were considerably more rugged. The campus was set up to be a bit rustic to simulate life as we might experience it on the mission field. Laundry rooms had the old ringer washers and wash tubs, restrooms and showers were down the hall, and running water meant we ran down stairs with a bucket to get water.

Courses included New Testament Church, culture, practical class, hold the ropes, and daily chapel. Each class was designed to give us the tools we would need to plant a Church in a remote location with an indigenous people group. More than mere instruction, we were taking the principles learned in class and practicing them in a simulated environment. In one of the simulations, I was teaching a Bible lesson to classmates who were playing the part of tribal villagers. One of my classmates decided to be a disruptive tribal leader. The disruptive part, he did rather well, but on all accounts got a bit carried away in his performance when he took my teaching notes, crumpled them up, and gave them a toss. It was hard to know at that point if he was playing the part of a tribal leader or making a personal point that I should not be using notes. Regardless, what do you do? Keep teaching? That was the point of the simulation! Take the situation as it presents itself and make a decision. I chose to continue with the lesson. After the simulation, we reviewed the events as a class and discussed what worked and what didn't work.

There was more to the missions training experience than classwork. When we signed up for the training, we agreed not to have an outside job for the year so that we could devote ourselves fully to the training. We had classes in the morning and work detail in the afternoon. That first semester work detail was wholly devoted to wood crew. The camp had natural gas for heat but relied on it only as the backup system. To save money all the buildings on campus were heated by wood burning boilers. Our task as students was to supply the boilers with wood. It was our fortune as a camp that a huge tornado had ripped through the area just a couple years prior. According to those who lived in the area, the twister touched down at an adult entertainment establishment totally destroying it, cut a path a half-mile wide through the country side, and lifted up after demolishing a liquor store. I'm not sure how much the story had grown by the time I heard it, but I saw the half-mile wide path it had cut. It left an impressive mess where we spent a great deal of time in gathering wood for the boilers. Before winter arrived, we had gathered, chopped, and stacked 250 full cord of wood.

Processing and stacking wood wasn't only about supplying fuel for the boilers. It was time that we spent together as men — staff and students doing life together. The work was exhausting and at times our tempers flared. Talk about practical class! We learned how to apply principles from the Word like *agree to disagree* and *deal with anger before the sun goes down*. Literally!

One positive lesson I remember came while I was splitting wood with Dan Stokes, one of the instructors. Dan turned to me and asked, "Tim, how do you suppose God would have you split that log?" What I wanted to say was, "Hmm–let me see, Dan. I stand the log up, swing this sixteen-ounce mall really hard, and split it into two pieces!" Instead, I stepped back and said, "I hadn't given it much thought." Dan did two things in that moment. One, he suggested I ask God how He would split the wood and in doing so, taught me that God was interested in the details of my life–even splitting wood. Two, he showed me his secret to splitting wood which proved to be a smarter way rather than the harder way I had been doing it. Turns out there is a technique to splitting wood.

In moments like those with Dan on wood crew, I was experiencing what Jesus meant when he said, "Make disciples." I had personally studied and preached messages using those words. But, there was so much more to making disciples than studying or preaching a message. Making disciples was going to involve living life with others.

We Could Never Do That!

Oddly enough, it was a couple decades after missions training before I would travel overseas. In that time of waiting, I had plenty of opportunities to live life with other believers in the work place and church. The most memorable discipleship-making times took place in our local church, working with the youth. We purposed from the first gathering to involve our young people in planning and leading their program. Every aspect was completely theirs to plan and manage–music, topics, activities, and snacks. Now, I clearly loved teaching and regularly shared from the Word, but I purposed to give our young people the opportunity to share the things they were learning from Scripture. I wanted them to develop their own love for God's Word and be comfortable sharing with others.

The Lord eventually gave me opportunities to travel overseas. Most of my trips are short making the *living life together* approach to discipleship impossible. It has not however hindered me from practicing the "teaching them to obey all things" aspect of Jesus' words.

On a recent trip to Myanmar, I had the privilege of working with pastors, church leaders, and seminary instructors from three different language groups to review key passages in their recently completed New Testaments. Our goal was to determine if their translations clearly communicated the author's intended message. The group appreciated the tool we shared with them for reviewing the passages. They asked for printed copies of all the content we had developed to-date and suggested that we create more content. Of course, we were willing to create more, but I had just shared Matthew 28:18-20 with them in one of the daily devotionals. Jesus' words were still on my mind, "teach them to obey all things". So, I said, "You guys are pastors and seminary teachers. You don't have to wait for us to develop more content. Use what we've given you as a starting point. You develop content too. Share your work with us and together we will be helping others review their Bible translations."

I continued the thought with another question, "Are there others that you know who speak a different language that need Scriptures translated?"

"Yes", they answered.

"What will you do to help them translate the Bible into their languages?"

"We will bring them to you so that you can teach them how to do Bible translation."

"That's fine, but we can only train so many language groups in a year. You told us that there are 200 or more languages here in Myanmar that need Scriptures translated. What if you started teaching others how to do Bible translation? Then we would be multiplying our efforts."

"We could never do that!"

Tabitha, my colleague, spoke up, "When you came to your first Bible translation workshop, how many of you said you could not translate Scripture?" They all raised their hands. "And, yet you have translated the entire New Testament and some of you have completed the Old Testament."

"If you train us, then we will be able teach others how to do Bible translation." They agreed.

It was a shorter *living life together* approach to making disciples than what I learned in missions training or practiced with the youth. But, we had been part of sharing an incredible gift with these dear brothers and sisters in Christ—the gift of translating God's Word into the language of their birth. It seemed appropriate to encourage them as our disciples to go and do the same.

Prayer

Lord, thank you for putting others in my life to disciple me.
Lord, use me to disciple others.

Chapter Seven

Ministry Detour

Verse
*Whatever you do, work at it with all your heart,
as working for the Lord...
Colossians 3:23*

Introduction

With a year of missions training complete, it was time to pack up our belongings and move to a new location for the next phase of training. NTM's language school was in Camdenton, MO, on the shores of the beautiful Lake of the Ozarks. Our first time driving to the school was an adventure. The school had a sign out at the main road with instructions that said, "Turn right at the next road." We turned at the next road, which appeared like any other, but a few hundred feet from the turn the road narrowed dramatically. It was technically a two-lane road; however, with a trailer in tow, I was glad we were the only ones driving down and around the winding curves. As we neared the end of that road, we saw the school's welcome sign indicating we had arrived, but this was only the main entrance to the property. We still had a little more driving to do. Now, we were winding down a slightly narrower gravel drive through a densely wooded area. We soon started seeing buildings and a great view of the lake. The school's dock and swimming area appeared in the distance. It reminded me of lakes back home and I remember thinking *This is going to be a nice place to wrap up our missionary training*.

After settling into our apartment and getting familiar with the area, we quickly shifted into a busy schedule of classes and work detail. The course

51

work was much more technical than our previous year. We were being trained in language and culture acquisition which included classes in phonetics, phonemics, and linguistics. Several of our instructors had field experience. Thus, they were skilled at showing us how to elicit needed information and catalogue it for future use in teaching and translating Scripture.

Jean Dye Johnson was one of our instructors who taught Bible translation methodology. Jean had acquired her training in linguistics by attending summer workshops decades before that eventually became known as the Summer Institute of Linguistics. She was highly regarded in NTM for her work as a Bible translator, but we knew of Jean because she had written a book that was required reading in our missions training. In her book, *God Planted Five Seeds,* Jean recounted the story of the first five NTM missionaries who were martyred by the very people group they were attempting to reach with the gospel. Her first husband was one of the five killed. It was an amazing story of how God used Jean and the other widows to eventually share the Word of God with that tribal group. It was a special privilege to receive instruction from someone of Jean's caliber and experience.

In one session, I remember Jean teaching us when it was appropriate to substitute words in the translation. She asked us, "How would you translate the phrase 'white as snow' for a group that never has and never will see snow?" Some said, "It must be translated 'white as snow'." Jean, in her gentle way, replied, "Would substituting a word for 'snow' really change the meaning of the text? Not really. This would actually be a place you could make a substitution like 'white as sand on the seashore'." This was revelatory to me as I had never considered substituting words when translating Scripture. Then she asked, "How would you translate the phrase 'Passover lamb' for a group that had never seen sheep? Could you for example, substitute the word 'pig' for 'lamb'?" The class was silent. Jean said, "In this case, a substitution would create issues with the cultural and historical context of the Scriptures. It would be important to keep the word 'lamb' in this phrase due to the significance sheep had in the Jewish culture and the sacrificial system established by God." I have never forgotten key principles on Scripture translation learned in her class, nearly 30 years ago.

How Flexible Are You?

Near the end of our training was a live language experience. This live language experience was the capstone to the language school course where we would apply all the things we learned in a full emersion situation. In years prior, students traveled to a Cherokee community and settled in for two weeks practicing language and culture acquisition with language helpers. We were to be the first class to travel to a new community of Hmong speakers. Naturally, we were looking forward to the experience. It would be a better indication of our language learning abilities then the classroom setting, and it would be the culmination of our four years of training. We would finally be missionaries ready to head to an overseas ministry.

One afternoon, shortly before we were to leave for the live language experience, my work detail supervisor tapped me on the shoulder and said, "Tim, the chairman wants to see you in his office." I thought to myself, *The school chairman wants to see me? Did we do something wrong?*

"How soon? Should I finish up what I'm doing, or does he want to see me now?"

"Now!" He responded.

"Okay." At that point, I was really feeling uncomfortable as I left what I was doing and walked over to the chairman's office. I waited outside his door as the receptionist let him know that I had arrived. The door opened and Dave Murray, the chairman, welcomed me in, offering me a seat across from his desk.

"Tim, how flexible are you?" He asked.

"I don't know–it depends I guess."

"NTM has a need for a branch bookkeeper at the Bible School in Jackson, MI. We thought you would be a good fit for the role and would like you to consider it."

"How soon?" I asked.

"Right away." He said.

"What about our training? We are almost done."

"They need you to make at least a two-year commitment. Since you will need a refresher course after two years anyway, it would be okay to leave without finishing the training. And, they need you right away. Go discuss it with Nancy and let me know what you decide."

Well, that was not at all what I expected! As I walked back to our apartment, I was thinking, *Nancy's dad was the bookkeeper at the Bible school in Jackson back when we were dating. He taught me how to do budgeting over the years. So, I do have a general understanding of how to keep track of spending. But bookkeeping at the Bible school? How do I even bring this up to Nancy? Her heart is set on going to the field.*

I walked into the apartment much earlier in the day than normal. Nancy was surprised to see me and asked, "Is everything okay?"

To which I replied, "Sweetheart, how flexible are you?"

"It depends. What did you have in mind?"

"We've been offered the bookkeeping position at the Jackson Bible school. If we say yes, it would be a two-year commitment."

"Seriously!" She exclaimed. "You know I really want to go to the field."

"As do I, but it's only two more years. I think we should accept. We can still go serve overseas after that."

We called our family, prayed about it, and together agreed to accept the offer – all within a couple of days. Once again, we were packing up our belongings. Only this time, we were on our way to Jackson, MI, to begin our first assignment as missionaries with NTM. It wasn't the assignment we had worked so hard preparing for, but above all we wanted to serve in whatever capacity God saw fit to use us. He seemed to be asking us to do bookkeeping for the next two years and we wanted to give it our best effort in keeping with Paul's instruction, "Whatever you do, work at it with all your heart, as working for the Lord…"

From Linguistics to Ledgers

One week Nancy and I were in language and linguistics class preparing for the live language experience. The next, we were unpacking our belongings at the Bible school in Jackson as the new bookkeeper. We barely had time to catch our breath from the move and we were sent off to NTM's corporate headquarters in Sanford, FL, for a crash course in accounting. The trip to Sanford worked out well for us as Neal, Nancy's dad, was one of my instructors. While I was being trained, Nancy and our daughter, Sarah, got to spend some time with Nancy's mom.

Neal was on NTM's internal audit team. He received his training in accounting from a CPA while serving overseas as a field bookkeeper. One of his responsibilities as an internal auditor was training others to be bookkeepers. Virgil Wuthrich, a CPA, was also on the internal audit team and another one of my instructors. Together, they gave me a two-week crash course in debits, credits, ledgers, subledgers, and journals of original entry. The text book was *Fundamentals of Accounting*. I still have my copy. They also introduced me to the accounting team at headquarters and gave me a complete overview showing me how my work as a branch bookkeeper would be rolled up into the corporate accounting records.

Two weeks of training would have to be sufficient as I was needed back in Jackson to take over for the outgoing bookkeeper. From that point forward, I would get on-the-job training with the active records. Neal traveled up from FL to take me through my first end-of-month process. He often reassured me, "There is no mistake you can make that we can't fix." I did make quite a few mistakes in those early days putting Neal's words to the test. But, he was right! When it came to accounting, my mistakes were easily corrected. What he failed to mention was the effort it would take to find some of those mistakes. I was working with a completely paper system with manual transaction postings and calculations. Receiving a payment from a student on their school bill included a hand-written receipt, a hand-written entry on the students subledger page, a hand-written entry in the cash receipts journal, and manual calculations to sum columns in both the students subledger page and cash receipts journal. The opportunity for error increased with each hand-written step. I remember looking for one mistake late into the evening and not being able to find it. The next morning, I had my assistant look at my work to see if she could see what I was missing. I'll never forget her question, "Was that supposed to be a 2 or a 7?" From that day forward, I have written my 7's with a dash through them.

While mistakes could be found and corrected, my pride was taking a hit. I tend to set pretty high goals for myself. The system was such that I couldn't meet my own goals, and making mistakes was personally frustrating. In time, I came to accept the fact that mistakes were going to happen, but I was driven to improve the process to minimize and eliminate the human error element wherever possible. I was fortunate to have a colleague with an interest in personal computers. He had an old 8086 with a 5.25" floppy drive and a 10-megabyte hard drive with Microsoft Works installed. After going through the tutorial for Works, I set up data-entry screens and reports to automate the cash receipting process. We still had to hand key information into the system, but all the calculations were done by the computer reducing the opportunities for error.

In addition to learning personal computing, Neal and others encouraged me to take classes and further develop my skills. I enrolled in a correspondence program and eventually earned an associate's degree in specialized business with an emphasis in accounting. The experience and education gave me a better understanding of accounting theory which enabled me to critically evaluate the processes that I had been taught and make improvements—not because anyone asked me to, but simply because it was a good thing to do. My thought was, *if God has led me to be a bookkeeper, I am going to do it with excellence working at it with all my heart.*

First and Second Timothy

Nearly four years had passed since accepting the branch bookkeeping position at the Bible school. The leadership team asked me to continue as the bookkeeper past the two-year commitment. Nancy was having health issues at the time. So, we agreed to stay. By that time, I had settled into a comfortable routine and gained enough efficiencies in the bookkeeping role to take on other responsibilities. I was providing oversight for the intermural program, mentoring a group of single men, teaching classes, and occasionally speaking in chapel. It was a job I had dreamed about having someday after serving on the mission field. But, it was happening now! I remember thinking, *I could be happy doing this the rest of my life*.

Then early in the fall semester of '93, NTM had an urgent need for an office manager at their corporate headquarters and they asked me to fill the role. It was a tough decision. I asked, "Lord, do you really want me to leave the Bible school? This is home. My family and friends are here. I love what I'm doing. Are you sure?" By this time in our lives, Nancy's health was spiraling downward. With Nancy's mom and dad living in Sanford and working at the headquarters, we felt a peace about taking the new position especially since it put Nancy close to her mom. When we told our 3 ½ year old daughter Sarah that we were moving, she cried. As her tears rolled down her cheeks, I started crying too. Peace some-times comes with a little pain. While it didn't necessarily make sense, we packed up our belongings and moved to Sanford, FL.

Tim Meisel was the assistant treasurer of NTM and my new super-visor. We quickly became good friends and often referred to each other as *First* and *Second Timothy*. Tim was covering the manager responsibilities until I arrived and settled into the role. He walked in the office with me on my first day and introduced me to the team. I remember being ner-vous that morning. Questions were swirling in my head. *Am I going to fit in? Will they like me? What should I do first?* The nerves and questions quickly faded when I saw the faces of friends from my graduating class at Bible school. My first day was a class reunion!

After the introductions, hugs, and warm greetings, it was time to get to work. The next few weeks I spent learning and documenting each pro-cess in the finance office. There was a lot to learn as the team was respon-sible for handling all the incoming contributions, maintaining multiple thousands of donor records, paying the bills for operating the headquarters, and processing the payroll for more than three thousand missionaries serving around the world.

Each team member had a unique role and responsibility. I spent time with everyone learning how to do their job and documenting all the required steps. In the process, I asked myself, "What can we do to make this more efficient?" One of the women on my team was responsible for preparing the check batches for deposit at the bank. She was good with an adding machine and made deposit prep look easy. I sat with her to learn the steps.

She took the first bundle of checks with the accompanying documents from donors and said, "First, we need to run an adding machine tape for all the donor remit devices."

"Okay, I got it"

"Next, we need to run two adding machine tapes on the stack of checks."

To clarify, I asked, "Two adding machine tapes for the checks? What's the purpose of the second tape?"

She said, "We need one tape for our records and another tape to send with the checks to the bank."

"That's it! No other purpose for the second tape?" I replied.

"No, that's it!"

After documenting the rest of the process, I immediately pulled out my office supply catalogue and ordered a box of carbonless two ply adding machine rolls.

Over time we made other procedural changes to gain efficiencies. Most of the changes were considerably more complex and costly than purchasing carbonless adding machine rolls. As technology advanced, we acquired equipment and software that eliminated several of the manual processes. Soon, hand keying information into the computer was replaced with bar code scanning and character recognition software. Bank deposits were made electronically instead of hand carrying them to the bank. Month end close was reduced from days to hours. It was a season of change, but the team rose to the occasion. We had some challenging days with all the changes, but we all genuinely cared for each other and worked with all our hearts for the Lord.

I have often taken Paul's instruction in Colossians 3:23 personally, but he was speaking to a group of believers when he said, "Whatever _you_ do, work at it with all _your_ heart..." This team taught me what it meant to work with all your heart for the Lord as a group.

Whatever You Do

"How flexible are you?" That innocent question from Dave Murray was meant to be a brief ministry detour, but it became a lifelong career for me in accounting and finance. Most of my experience in this field has been in the ministry context with a couple of years' experience in the private sector. Over time, I have helped churches with accounting needs, provided personal bookkeeping services to individuals, and built a complex for-profit structure with multiple operating entities in strategic locations around the world. I eventually completed the educational requirements and became a Certified Public Accountant.

Accounting became my platform for serving the Lord in ministry. I've applied myself and pursued it with excellence. Some say that I'm pretty good at what I do. Those who know me well though know that accounting is not my passion. But, it is what God has put in front of me to do and I have leaned into it with everything I've got just like Paul said. "Whatever you do, _work_ at it with _all_ your heart..."

There have been seasons of doubt and frustration when I have cried out to God saying, "Are you sure this is what I'm supposed to be doing with my life?" So far, He keeps giving me peace as if to say, "Yes, this is what I'm asking you to do–for Me." My only response can be, "Okay Lord! I will serve you in this way with my whole heart!"

Prayer

Lord, whatever You ask–let me do it with all my heart.

Chapter Eight

Give Thanks

Verse

Give thanks in all circumstances;
for this is God's will for you in Christ Jesus.
1 Thessalonians 5:18

Introduction

"You're a grandpa?" This is a question I often get when I speak about my grandkids. Nancy and I presently have four ranging from eight years-old down to almost two. Tristan is the oldest followed by Vanessa, then Kaitlyn, and Noah.

We've been privileged to have our kids settle near us giving us the joy of spending time with our grandkids. When we go to their house, Nancy will knock on the door with her special knock and you can hear the shouts from the other side of the door, "Grandma's here!" Once in a while, I will show up at the house without grandma and use her special knock. It works every time, "Grandma's here!" Tristan and Vanessa are usually the first to reach the door. When they see it's me, they say "Grandpa, you shouldn't use grandma's knock." Kaitlyn will usually show up for a grandpa hug. Within seconds the little guy, Noah, comes barreling down the hall wrapping his one-and-a-half year old frame around my legs saying, "Papa, up!" Well, sometimes he says, "Papa, down!" But, he means up.

They each have their own personalities. Tristan will often greet me with, "Grandpa, did you know what I was doing?" Then he shares something special that he has been working on. Vanessa will bounce up in my arms for a grandpa hug, "Do you want to play Barbies with me Grandpa?" Kaitlyn will often follow her grandpa hug with, "Tickle me Grandpa!" Noah is still learning his vocabulary, but his smile says – *come kick the ball with me Grandpa*.

When Kaitlyn was Noah's age, she loved being chased. "Get me Grandpa!" What was I to do? Of course, I gave chase. As I scooped her up in my arms, I'd say, "I got you!" In her sweet little voice, she'd say, "I got you!" But, who got who? While I had securely wrapped her up in my arms, it was pretty clear that Katy-K had gotten me.

In moments like these, love overflows and giving thanks comes so naturally. I often pray, "God, thank you for my grandkids."

Why This? Why Now?

As missionaries with NTM, Nancy and I were required to raise financial support to fund our ministry. The support covered our salary, taxes as self-employed ministers, and benefits. NTM had recommended amounts to raise based on your service location and family size. The amounts were recommendations, meaning we were not required to raise the full amount before engaging in the ministry. It was difficult to raise support for a stateside role. Most folks we invited to join our financial support team felt that stateside roles should be paid positions instead of support based. In sixteen years with NTM, our support peaked at 35% of the recommended amount. It was a meager lifestyle, but the Lord faithfully provided finances at just the right time to meet our needs. In fact, we managed to navigate that season of life without debt — not even a car payment.

We have heard amazing stories of God's financial provision over the years from other missionaries. I remember the story of one family sitting down for dinner with nothing more than a can of beans to share among the eight of them. After they prayed and thanked God for the meal, the doorbell rang. Friends from church who owned a catering business showed up and said, "Sorry to bother you this evening, but we had a last-minute cancelation on an order and you guys immediately came to mind." Instead of beans that night, the family enjoyed a Thanksgiving style feast with leftovers to spare.

Nancy and I didn't have experiences like sitting down to the table with our last can of beans to share as a family. We trusted the Lord for finances and provisions just the same, but He always seemed to meet our needs in advance. One summer, we considered enrolling our daughters in a local Christian school. The tuition was reasonable compared to other schools, but it was clearly beyond what we could afford. We were in the school office debating whether to sign the paperwork. Nancy said, "This seems like the right decision for the girls."

"I agree, but we've never committed to a payment we couldn't cover on our budget."

"Yes, I know. Do you think it's possible the Lord wants us to move forward anyway?" She asked.

"Well, I could be comfortable signing the registration and see if the Lord provides the funds before the school year begins. What do you think?"

"Yeah, that sounds reasonable." She said.

So, we signed the registration for the girls and before the school year began, the Lord provided the full amount for the tuition, books, and incidentals. God met our financial need in a way that made sense to us at the time.

In 2003, our funding was trending upward nearing 35% of the recommended amount. With encouragement and help from friends and family, we decided it was time to purchase a house. The housing market was prime for buyers and interest rates down near 4%. We ended up signing a contract on a new home in a subdivision near NTM's office. Our contract was in the first batch of houses to be built and in just six short months we moved into our first house as a family.

I remember that first night settling into sleep and whispering, "Nancy, listen! Do you hear that?"

She said, "Hear what?"

I answered, "Exactly!" It was completely quiet. No sounds of televisions or radios, kids rough housing, tooth brushes tapping on sinks — there were no sounds of any kind coming from neighboring apartments. It was amazing!

Shortly after moving into our new home, we started receiving word from some of our financial supporters and it wasn't good. One after another wrote of their need to reduce or cut their financial support all together. The reasons were understandable — failed business, divorce, death. Within four weeks, our funding dropped more than $500 a month.

I remember thinking, *how can this be? The Lord seemed to have put all the pieces in place for us to buy this house. Why this? Why now?* We were facing other life challenges as well — challenges that were big enough to cause us to question whether to continue ministering with NTM. It was a difficult time. We had committed our lives to the ministry with NTM right out of high school. With four years of training and six-teen years of service, I just assumed we would be with NTM until we retired. But, there we were, struggling—and on top of that—the loss of financial support. Giving thanks in that circumstance was the furthest thing from my mind.

White Shirts and Leather Sole Shoes

"Sitting for the CPA exam? Really? I would have guessed a pastor or counselor. Wow, an accountant!" These were the words of a classmate of mine at my 25th high school class reunion. Truth is, I wouldn't have guessed accountant either, but it was true. The journey to CPA status had begun five years before that reunion when we had left NTM.

The loss of financial support was the final piece that convinced us that it was time to leave NTM. A local accounting firm in the Orlando area just happened to be taking applications. This was no ordinary firm in that their mission was to provide accounting services exclusively to non-profit organizations and their subsidiaries. I applied for a position thinking, *if I must leave NTM, this job would at least give me an oppor-tunity to serve a broader group of ministries.*

I was offered the job and started as a staff accountant in the Spring of 2006. It was a completely new experience. The dress code was profes-sional. Guys were to wear white shirts (starched), silk ties (not too busy), dark suits, leather sole shoes, and be clean shaven. The nice clothes were no problem but shaving off my mustache was tough. I had worn a mus-tache since the day I could grow one and my girls, both teenagers, had never seen me without facial hair. The firm made a temporary exception allowing me to keep the mustache until after my daughter's wedding which took place just a few weeks after my start date.

In addition to the dress code, I was learning to manage my time more rigidly. We were required to record our work in ten-minute increments as our time was billable. Staff accountants were required thirty-five billable hours a week. I had no idea what that meant when I started, but it didn't take me long to figure out that I had to work considerably more than forty hours a week to accumulate the billable minimum.

One morning during my first week on the job, the managing partner invited me to his office for a meeting. He said, "Tim, we would like you to work on the tax side of the practice."

"Tax? Are you sure? I'm not that familiar with tax and think audit would be a better fit." I replied.

"The tax partner really needs help, and I think you are the right person for the job."

"Okay, I'll give it my best effort."

The next few months, I plunged into non-profit tax work preparing Federal and State forms for clients, doing research, and writing technical documents. It wasn't all that difficult, but it was detailed and time consuming. Time became a major issue for me in that we were given time budgets for each of the tax projects. For example, we were given an eight-hour budget to prepare an information return, Federal Form 990, for clients. Not all Form 990's are created equal and I rarely managed to complete one within the budgeted time. This led to another conversation with the managing partner.

"Tim, you do great work. But, it is taking way too long."

"I understand. If it helps, I can stop counting hours once I get to the budget time." I offered.

"No, we really want to know how long it takes to complete these tasks." I later discovered that some of the other staff accountants were doing exactly what I offered. They stopped counting their hours when they reached the budgeted time even though it was taking them much longer to complete the work. He continued, "We want to send you out with the audit teams to see if that might be a better fit."

So, I continued with some tax work and added audit to my schedule. It was nice getting out of the office for a change and spending time with clients. Audit work felt like a better fit to me. About the time I was beginning to feel comfortable with the new routine, my teammate who had just finished a phone call leaned over to me and said, "You're needed back at the office." It was four in the afternoon on a Friday and I was at a client's office. I thought, *what could be so important that I was needed back at the office at this hour.*

The managing partner was waiting for me in his office. He invited me in, closed the door behind me, and had me sit down across from his desk. "Tim, I don't know a better way to say this, but it's just not working out."

I was not expecting that! "Even audit?" I asked.

"Yeah, even audit. I am sorry. I've discussed this with the partners and we have agreed to allow you to stay on with us for thirty more days while you look for another job."

I thanked him for allowing me to continue working as that was not the firm's normal practice. We stood, shook hands, and I left for the day.

That was the longest drive home in my life. I called Nancy while on the way to let her know what happened and managed somehow to keep my composure until I got to the house. She greeted me at the door with a reassuring embrace. It was good she was holding me because I was emotional at that point and felt all the strength leave my body.

Give thanks in this circumstance? This is God's will? The grief was so intense that I had chest pains. I wasn't thankful for what was happening and could not see how it could possibly be God's will for my life—not at that time and not while I was experiencing such pain. Still, I knew I had to finish well. The following Monday, I arrived at the office like before only this time hurting deeply, but ready to be a testimony to my coworkers of how to honor God when life didn't make sense.

Integrity Matters

Finding a job in thirty days or less was not an easy task. The difficulty was compounded by the fact that I was seriously depressed. My first interview was with a recruiter at a placement agency that specialized in helping accounting professionals find jobs. The recruiter wrapped up the interview with, "I can see that you are struggling. You look depressed and defeated."

I wanted to say, *No kidding! What part of my explanation for needing a job did you miss?* Instead, I replied, "Yeah, everyone tells me I'm an easy person to read."

He continued, "I know your experience was tough. But, here's the thing. This interview did not go well and I'm not going to be able to recommend you to any of my clients."

"What? I need a job! What do you suggest I do?"

"Well, I would suggest that you take some time to recover before you go to another interview because no one is going to hire you right now."

It was a nice thought but taking time to recover was clearly not an option. My family was counting on me to find a job. So, I continued applying for jobs and going to interviews. By God's grace, within two-weeks' time, I had two job offers and started work in a new position as a controller for a local printing company. The transition was quick enough that I didn't miss a paycheck. I was thankful to have a job, but it would be months before I recovered from the depression.

I was now working in the private sector managing an accounting team that covered inventory, work in process, commission-based sales, standard billable rates, payables, receivables, collections, and reporting. There was a slight learning-curve, but the accounting side of the job was easy enough to grasp. What I lacked in practical experience for the job, I made up for in book knowledge as I quickly adjusted to the new routine.

The biggest learning curve came with the managerial duties. With less than two weeks on the job, my boss asked me into his office for a meeting. He said, "I want you to reduce the accounting team from seven to three."

I laughed and said, "Are you being serious?"

"This is no joke. I want you to cut the team to three. I'll give you four weeks to get it done."

"Wow! I barely know the team and my initial assessment on the work load is that there are at minimum four full-time positions not including myself."

"Okay." He said. "Cut the team to four including yourself in the next four weeks."

Apparently, I was hired to completely reconstruct the accounting function because it was going to require significant changes in processes to cut three full-time positions without creating an enormous amount of work for the remaining team members. The task and the timeline felt impossible, but I had my instructions and got to work reviewing all the processes to see where we could make changes. I sat with each team member, observed their routines, and documented procedures. The procedures for one of the jobs included many unnecessary steps. I thought to myself, *this person has figured out how to take a 20-hour position and cram it into a 42-hour week.*

By the end of the four weeks, I made changes to the office procedures, updated performance goals and measures, shifted some of the work to my desk, and reduced the team from seven to four. Those were hard days as I was the one sitting across the desk from good people letting them know that their jobs were ending. While a painful reminder of my recent experience, I gained a greater appreciation for clearly written and implemented performance goals and measures. Now, my team understood the expectations for their jobs and I had an objective way to evaluate their performance.

Over the next few months, other departments were going through similar exercises to cut costs and improve the company's profitability. The changes in accounting alone should have created a noticeable difference in the bottom line, but we were still experiencing losses. I started taking a closer look at the financial reports and comparing line items like inventory and work in process (WIP) with my own counts. As I dug into the details, I found inconsistencies that I brought to the attention of my boss. "I think we have a serious problem. It appears as though we have items listed in WIP from jobs that were completed several months ago."

"I'm aware of that situation." He replied.

"What caused it? Why wasn't it cleaned up before now?"

"We approach reporting a little differently..." He began.

The explanation that followed made me uncomfortable because the approach failed to fit with reporting standards and required a significant deviation from generally accepted accounting principles. I expressed concern to my boss and others in positions of authority. When nothing was done to correct the situation, I was forced to make a choice; do my job as instructed or look for another job. I chose to look for another job in order to maintain my own personal integrity.

Playing Basketball

Discouraged, depressed, disillusioned would have been accurate words to describe how I felt. In less than three-years, we had left the ministry with NTM, I had lost a job I really enjoyed, and now I was in a job requiring actions that conflicted with my conscience. Intellectually, I knew God had a plan and that I could trust Him. Emotionally, I was struggling. It was easy giving thanks when the circumstances were good. But, things were not good, and I was not thankful for the position I was in or for the circumstances that led to it. As for God's will, I was at a complete loss. It seemed God was leading in each decision, but how could any of this have been God's will for my life?

Well, God did have a plan and His will in the circumstances started coming into focus the Summer of 2008. I received a text from my father-in-law mentioning a job posting that I should check out. The posting was a Vice President of Finance position for Wycliffe Associates (WA). I clicked the link and sent in my resume. Within a couple of hours of hitting the send button, an email popped up in my in-box from Bruce Smith the President of WA. He introduced himself, sent a few preliminary questions, mentioned he was traveling in Asia, and that he would like to meet me as soon as he returned. I agreed, and we set a time to meet.

As I pulled up to the WA building, I saw a tall gentleman standing out near the flag pole. It was Bruce. When I stepped out of my car, he introduced himself and said, "You can leave your coat and tie in the car. Make yourself comfortable. We're less formal here." I took my coat and tie off and followed him into the building. He led me up the stairs to a conference room on the second floor. With a whiteboard at his back and a marker in his hand, the interview began.

"Tell me a little more about yourself." He said. I shared my testimony and some of my experience in ministry with NTM. Then he asked the most unusual question, "So, do you like basketball or football?"

Thinking this was still in the "getting to know you" category, I answered, "I like watching football, but definitely prefer playing basketball."

Then Bruce explained, "Several organizations are like football teams. They huddle up to talk about the play, line up on the line of scrimmage, fall forward a couple of feet, and then huddle up to talk about the next play. WA is not a football team. We play basketball. Everyone knows their position and is in the right place at the right time. And, we only call time-outs to discuss things as needed." From that point, Bruce shared the history of WA and cast a vision for where the organization was headed. We wrapped up the meeting and before I got home an email with an offer was waiting for me in my in-box.

I accepted the offer and have now been a "basketball player" with WA for more than ten years. Over these years, I have found that everything I experienced in that difficult season between NTM and WA was preparation for the work at WA. The effort at NTM improving the processes and reducing the month-end close from days to hours was exactly what WA needed. My new team in 2008 was processing gifts manually and taking ten business days or more to close month-end. It was like I stepped back in time to 1993 at NTM for a complete "do over." The tax research at the accounting firm was exactly what WA needed. At the time, WA was filing information returns with the IRS, pension and benefit forms with the Department of Labor, and solicitation registrations for various States. With a few adjustments in our status with the IRS, we were able to make use of exemptions eliminating the unnecessary work load and associated cost of all those filings. The work I had done at the print shop updating performance goals and measures was also exactly what was needed at WA. Time is a precious resource that should not be wasted especially in non-profit organizations like WA.

Looking back, it is easy to see that God had a plan and everything I experienced was indeed His will for my life. I wish I would have been able to thank Him as I was going through the disappointment and pain. While I want to believe that I have learned that valuable life lesson, I can only pray that He will remind me to be thankful in all circumstances knowing that it is His will for my life.

Prayer

Lord, remind me to be thankful in all circumstances, even the bad ones. Lord, remind me that Your plan and will for my life is good.

Chapter Nine

Lessons in Leadership

Verse

...in humility consider others better than yourselves. Each of you should look not only to your own interests, but also to the interests of others.
Philippians 2:3-4

Introduction

"You should run for student council president." Mr. Barsuhn my high school class advisor suggested. I had served for a year on the council as a class representative in the past but had never considered running for president.

"Me? Run for president?"

He said, "Yeah! You have the needed leadership qualities and I think you would do a great job."

Mr. Barsuhn's opinion meant a lot to me since he had been our class advisor since the seventh grade. I especially looked up to him because he was an exceptional teacher bringing subjects like history and literature to life for me. These were subjects I had struggled with in times past, but he had a way of making learning fun. It wasn't just sitting through a lecture and hoping I jotted down the right information for a test. From the time we walked into his classroom until the bell rang signaling the end of class, Mr. Barsuhn drew us into conversations and took us on journeys that felt like his own personal discoveries. Beyond the classroom, he spent time with us showing genuine care for us as individuals not just students.

Mr. Barsuhn's encouragement was all I needed to step up and run for president. I gathered the required number of signatures from my class-mates and others of the student body. On election day, the candidates gave speeches. I don't remember much about the content of my speech, but I do remember an upper classman's critique. He said, "You leaned on the podium and you crossed your legs while you were speaking. Oh, and you said 'um' a lot." I didn't know how to respond and simply said, "Okay. Thanks for the feedback." Apparently, my presentation wasn't too distracting as I was elected student council president.

Student council was responsible for organizing and hosting various events during the school year. The biggest one of the year was home-coming. It was more than a single event as there were activities to plan for every day of the week leading up to and including homecoming day. The idea of the week was to have fun as a student body and build school spirit. We had special dress up days and closed out the week with a pep rally. First thing Saturday morning, we had a parade with floats representing each class that traveled busy streets with police escort from our school to the stadium where the big game would be played later that morning. Then that evening, we hosted a formal banquet where the homecoming king and queen were crowned. It was a busy week for students, families, and faculty in general, but for those of us on student council and our advisors it was crazy busy!

All in all, Mr. Barsuhn's encouragement led me into a great first experience in leadership. The work was beyond anything a single person could manage on his own. It required planning and assigning tasks to team members that included acquiring permits, securing venues, hiring caterers, and laying out action steps for each day of the week. When homecoming finally arrived, we successfully executed the plan giving our fellow students, parents, and faculty an amazing week.

Caring Is Contagious

Self-help books written about leadership are abundant. They cover things like influencing and inspiring teams to do great things. I have my favorite writers on the topic and have learned much by reading the experiences of other leaders. But one quality that I have attempted to put into practice didn't come from a self-help book. It's a quality that Mr. Barsuhn demonstrated during those high school days — a quality that Paul described to the believers at Philippi when he said, "…in humility consider others better than yourself…look not only to your own interests, but also to the interests of others." That quality is genuine care for others.

This verse had a profound influence on me as I took my first official leadership position. I was 25 years old when I stepped into the finance office manager position at NTM's corporate headquarters. As mentioned previously, I knew some of the team members from Bible school days, but most only knew me as the new boss. Some even referred to me as "the boss" which felt uncomfortable to me because it seemed to convey that I was there to tell everyone what to do whether they liked it or not. While I likely had that level of authority, I wanted to be known as more than a boss to my team. I wanted to be a leader and Paul's words seemed to indicate that a leader is someone who puts the needs of others ahead of his own. A leader is someone who genuinely cares for his team.

My priority was learning and documenting everyone's job. It was the perfect opportunity to spend time with each member of the team hearing their life stories and discovering in casual conversation things they considered important. I remember sitting at the data key station with Charlotte saying, "I notice you're wearing a wrist brace. Are you experiencing pain?"

"Occasionally." She said. "I decided to wear the brace regularly to avoid surgery."

There must be more to the story, I thought to myself. "So, does anyone else know how to data key?"

"Yes, Barbara knows how to data key. She used to do this job before me. I took over after her carpel tunnel surgery." She replied.

"That's quite a stack of boxes you've got behind you. I'm assuming they all need to be data keyed."

"Correct!"

"Well, I'm here to learn. So, teach me how to data key and then I will take a couple of those boxes back to my desk to practice."

From that day forward, I walked back to Charlotte's workstation and grabbed a box or two to help lighten her load just a little. She would often say, "You don't have to do that. You've got too many other things to do."

"I know, but I like data keying and I like helping when I can."

On the other end of the office Barbara was busy preparing bundles of checks for the daily bank deposit. I made my way over to her work station and said, "Barb, it's time for me to learn how to prepare bank deposits. Are you ready to teach me how this works?"

She was a quiet person and in her soft voice said, "Sure, pull up a chair."

71

With note pad in hand, I began jotting down each of the steps as she explained them to me. In the hour of time I spent with her, other members of the team dropped by the work station putting bundles of checks in the bin for processing. At the end of the day, others on the team filed out for the evening having completed their work. Barbara stayed to prepare the last of the check bundles for deposit.

I said, "Barb, what would you think if I took a couple of these bundles to help you finish up?"

"That would be great! I could sure use the help."

In the days that followed, I made sure to stop by Barb's workstation to help her finish processing the check bundles for deposit so that she could finish the day with everyone else.

As I learned each person's role in the office, I looked for ways to express my care without saying a word. It wasn't always about doing the work. Sometimes expressing care meant paying attention to little things like noticing that the coffee was nearly gone or that the temperature in the room was too hot or too cold. I wasn't a coffee drinker at the time, but I learned how to brew coffee so that I could serve my team.

The day eventually came when it was time to make changes in our processes—the day when I would need to do the bosses duty of instructing the team in what we were going to do moving forward. As I shared about team work and cross training, everyone had seen me modeling it for them. While some were skeptical at first, they knew that I cared for each of them and that I wouldn't ask them to do anything I wasn't willing to do myself. In a relatively short period of time, I started seeing team members finish their work and instead of leaving for the day they would wander over to Charlotte's workstation to grab a box to data key or to Barb's workstation to lend a hand in finishing up the days deposits—not because I told them, but because I showed them.

We made some incredible advancements in our daily process. The most rewarding for me was that we became a team that genuinely cared for each other.

It Involves Listening

My leadership responsibilities eventually expanded beyond the finance office. NTM had a leadership team at the corporate office that provided oversight to the entire headquarters operations with nearly 80 staff serving in several different departments. By the time I reached the age of 30, I had been asked to be the chairman of that leadership team and assumed the director of operations duties.

In my new role, I primarily worked with a group of managers who were leading teams like the one I had led in the finance office. But, the role expanded my team from 8 to 80 and I quickly had a greater number of people stopping by my office asking, "You got a minute?" As often as I have been asked that question, the conversations that followed have rarely taken a minute or less. Two guys frequently came by to ask me if I had a minute.

One tended to stop by to express a frustration or concern. In one of those *got-a-minute* conversations, he said, "Tim, one of my coworkers is making it difficult for me to do my job."

"Have you talked to him about what's making it difficult?" I asked.

"I wanted to, but he is not someone I feel comfortable approaching."

"Let's say things were reversed. How would you want someone to handle the situation if you were the one being difficult?"

"Yeah, I would definitely want them to come to me first. Like I said, I really wanted to go to him first."

"Okay. So, how would you approach him? What would you say?"

From there, he explained how he envisioned a conversation. As it turned out, he had a well thought out approach for having the conversation. I said, "Man, that sounds like a great way to handle it. Give it try and let me know how it goes." We had some follow up discussions as he worked through the issue with his coworker. In those *got-a-minute* conversations, I spent a good bit of time just listening. And, that is basically all he needed—someone to listen and provide a caring word of encouragement to follow through on what he already knew he needed to do.

The other guy who stopped by often came with a new idea or creative thought that he had to share. He would start with, "Tim, is it a good time? I know you got a lot goin' on. This will only take a minute."

I just smiled and said, "Come on in. My time is yours. What's on your mind?" Some of the ideas shared were great, others, not so much. Some ideas were beyond my scope of authority. Regardless, I enjoyed the opportunity to hear his thoughts. One time he stopped by with that urgent look on his face and I knew this conversation was going to take some time. He said, "Tim, you know, this building here is like our home." The reality is that it was both our place of work and our home because the 2nd and 3rd floors of the building were staff apartments.

He said, "When people come here to visit the office, they are coming to our home and they need to feel welcome."

"I totally agree with you! How are we failing to make people feel welcome?" I asked.

"Look! Right out there!" He was pointing out my office window at the parking area in front of our building.

"Okay. What am I supposed to be seeing?"

"Parking spaces!" He said. "We don't have any visitor parking spaces! How are visitors supposed to feel welcome if they drive up and there's no place for them to park? I think we need to mark off a few spaces for visitors—right up near the door."

"I think you're right! That would be a nice way to help our visitors feel welcome."

It was a relatively simple thing, but one that was clearly not on my to-do list. In fact, it was an item for our facilities manager to consider rather than me. But, there I was receiving a passionate presentation on visitor parking spaces. I loved it! The idea and the passion! In that conversation and others that would follow I found another guy that just needed someone who would listen—even if the response wasn't favorable.

I cannot say that I always responded well to the *got-a-minute* requests. Sadly, there were times I thought to myself *no, I don't got a minute— please go away.* However, it was in those minutes that I learned how to prefer others by giving my time and often simply listening. It was a seemingly small yet meaningful way to prefer others and genuinely care for their needs.

Being Present

I have been the Vice President of Finance with WA for ten years. In that time, my responsibilities have grown beyond the duties at the corporate office in Orlando. I had teams and team members located around the world supporting WA's efforts in advancing Bible translation. That meant more travel time away from the office and when in the office considerably more time devoted to other tasks.

With the added responsibilities, I had to delegate several duties that were once part of my daily routine. This was tough because it meant I would have even less time or reason to connect directly with some of my team members in the office. Everyone knew that I had an open-door policy. In fact, the only time my door was closed was when I was on the phone or when a group discussion outside my door had risen to the level of distraction. The problem for me with the open-door policy was that it put all the effort to connect with me on everyone else. I had always been more actively involved with my teams and preferred to be the one creating the opportunities to connect.

One thing I continued doing while in the office was to periodically stop by to see various team members. It was appropriate to occasionally stretch my legs and give my eyes a break from the computer screens. So, I would make productive use of the time by checking in with folks. One team that got a little extra attention was the donor services team. They handled all the incoming contributions for WA and depending on the week or time of day would be intensely processing gifts.

"Hey everyone! Needed an eye break. So, thought I would come down and interrupt you guys."

They generally greeted me with, "How's your day going? Any exciting trips planned?" Occasionally the response was, "We're slammed." I knew to keep it short and let the team press on with their work. As often as possible though, I would attempt to leave the room having had a good laugh.

I remember one busy season where I had apparently missed a few days of dropping in on the team. One of the gals from donor services stopped by my office. She asked, "Is this a good time?"

"It is indeed. Please have a seat. What can I do for you?"

She said, "I don't know quite how to ask this, but have we done something wrong? Are you unhappy with us?"

"No. I think you guys are doing a great job. Why would you think that?" I asked.

"Well, you haven't been stopping by to see us lately and we were getting concerned."

I smiled and said, "Thank you for noticing. I am sorry that my busyness gave you that impression."

It was a welcome reminder to me that my stretch breaks and stopping by the team's office communicated that I cared. I very gladly resumed my habit of taking a break from the computer to interrupt the team from time to time.

In addition to communicating care, my showing up periodically created a level of comfort for folks to come and talk with me about hard things. I remember another team member coming to my office to confront me for something I said in a meeting. One of the ladies in the office came and said, "Tim, what you said in the meeting earlier today was really hurtful. You are like a little brother to me and I just knew I had to come and talk to you about this."

"Wow! I am so sorry that what I said came across that way. That is not at all what I meant. Please forgive me." I didn't remember saying what she brought to my attention, and to hear that my words had been hurtful was disappointing. I thrive on words of encouragement and as such do my best to use my words to encourage others. So, to hear that I had failed one of my team members in this way was tough. But, I was so glad that she considered me family and that she came.

I'm encouraged when my team reciprocates by checking in on me or when I see them checking in on each other. Being present and showing interest in the everyday activities proved to be an effective way to demonstrate genuine care even if I couldn't participate in doing the work like I had been able to in the past.

Change—The One Constant

Preferring others and genuinely caring for their needs in my decision making seemed to come more naturally for me. Even as a teen, I put a lot of effort into pleasing others in my decision-making. My stepdad often told me, "You can't please all the people all the time, only some of the people some of the times. You will drive yourself crazy trying." Over the years, I have learned to recognize the difference between pleasing others and preferring them. But, there was an aspect of preferring others that I had not considered until recently.

I've been privileged to have several mentors in my life. God has put men and women in my life at just the right time to influence my professional development directly or indirectly. My boss, Bruce Smith, has been one of my mentors encouraging me to continue improving. For example, I didn't need to be a CPA to do my job, but it was something I felt important for the role. Bruce encouraged me to keep going and made it part of my performance goals to show his support. Then as the finance guy, I clearly didn't need a PhD in Biblical studies to do my job, but it was something I felt compelled to pursue on a personal level. When I discussed it with Bruce, he encouraged me and supported the idea. He even brought up ways that my doctoral program could be a blessing to WA and added performance goals to motivate me to press on.

In WA, change is the one constant that we have come to expect—change for the sake of improving our ability to advance Bible translation. 2017 brought several changes to my area of responsibility. With the changes, I experienced a few challenges. One afternoon, Bruce and I were reviewing some of the details. He wasn't there to tell me what to do. In fact, I had learned in our ten years of working together that he expected me to make the decisions. He did however offer some words of wisdom when he said, "You can control things, and achieve only what you can do on your own. Or, you can allow others to make decisions and achieve more."

"That makes sense. It has always been my practice to delegate authority and decision-making." I said.

"But, do you prefer their decisions over your own?" He asked. While that sank in, he went on, "What if they make decisions different then you? The reality is that they will make decisions different then you. My experience is that others often make better decisions than I would."

That conversation caused me to look at preferring others in a new way. I had always connected preferring others with my decision making, but now I would look for ways to prefer others through their decision making. It didn't take long to put this new thought into practice. A team member stopped by my office to ask for advice. "Tim, this is awkward, but I feel like we just approved something that we should not be doing." When I heard the details, I thought *that is definitely not the way I would have handled it*. Bruce's words immediately came to mind—*prefer the decisions of others*.

"Do you think this will cause a tax issue?" I asked.

"Not to my knowledge."

"Yeah, I don't see it causing a problem with reporting either."

From there, I went on to share what I had been learning about preferring the decisions of others even when their decisions differ from my own decision-making.

There have been decisions I've had to step in and correct that conflict with tax and reporting standards. That is part of the job in leading others. But, there are several decisions each day that happen without me. Preferring those decisions over my own has enabled my team to do considerably more than could have been done if it was dependent on me.

More importantly, I have learned to apply Paul's instructions in a whole new way, "...in humility consider others better than yourselves. Each of you should look not only to your own interests, but also to the interests of others." My preference and genuine care for others has expanded to a deeper level.

Prayer

Lord, thank you for showing me how to genuinely care for others in decision making.

Lord, continue teaching me how to genuinely prefer the decisions of others.

Chapter Ten

Empowering Churches

Verse

His (God's) intent was that now, through the church, the manifold wisdom of God should be made known... Ephesians 3:10

Introduction

New Testament Church was an important topic in our training with NTM. If we were going to be church planters, we needed to understand the essential aspects of a church.

When I saw *New Testament Church* listed as a course for Bible school, I thought, *this should be an easy class. I've grown up in church and have a good idea what a church should look like.* I was in for a surprise!

The instructor began one discussion by asking, "When should the believers gather for worship?" I thought, *that's easy—of course they should meet on Sunday.* But, I wasn't about to answer because it felt like a trick question.

After an uncomfortable silence, someone spoke up, "Sunday."

"Okay, why Sunday?" The instructor replied.

"Because that was the day the Lord rose from the grave. It's His day."

"Sounds reasonable, but is there clear instruction in Scripture that churches need to meet on Sunday or is it tradition?" He asked. At that point, I was starting to feel a little offended by the implication that a church might not gather for worship on Sunday. Then he asked, "What if the believers choose to meet every night for worship after working all day in the fields? What's more important—the day and time? Or the gathering for worship?"

79

Many similar conversations followed in that class during the semester. Each challenged us to consider the differences between our traditional thinking and the teachings in Scripture about the local church.

We learned that a local church would demonstrate three essential characteristics — self-governing, self-supporting, and self-propagating. During one class discussion time the instructor asked, "What comes to mind when you think of the phrase self-governing?"

"Self-governing would indicate a local group of church leaders making decisions." Came one response.

"Elders and deacons as Paul described in Timothy and Titus providing spiritual leadership." Came another.

"Good! What about self-supporting?" He followed.

"That speaks to the issue of funding. So, that would mean the local church would be able to sustain itself financially." Someone suggested.

After a pause to allow for others to comment, the instructor said, "It is true that self-supporting includes local funding to sustain the ministry. But, it also includes local workers. It is important for the local believers to use their Spirit-given gifts and actively participate in the ministry of the church. Now, what about self-propagating?"

"Self-propagating means the local church will intentionally grow and produce other local churches."

"That is exactly right! It is the spiritual-multiplication principle that Jesus laid out when He said to make disciples of all nations."

These characteristics resonated with me because it was evident that we only had one life to offer. If a church that we planted was going to be successful, it would need to eventually function without us. That meant from day one, the work of planting a church needed to be focused on empowering local believers to do the ministry of the church not simply taking on the work ourselves. Paul modeled this for us as he traveled on his missionary journeys. Why did he do it that way? Because he understood that God's intent was to make His manifold wisdom known through the church. I was just starting to see the importance of Paul's words when it came to empowering the church to fulfill God's intent.

What About Quality?

While Nancy and I never had the privilege of going to the foreign field and planting a local church, many of our classmates from Bible school did. We often received updates from places like Indonesia, Paraguay, and Papua New Guinea explaining how the local churches had grown into networks of churches. The networks reached beyond their own language groups by sending families from their communities out as missionaries to neighboring villages that spoke different languages. It was exciting to hear the stories of God working in and through the local churches and church leaders to equip believers for works of service.

The pioneering efforts of our faithful friends and earlier missionaries had successfully established local churches. These churches were empowered to lead, teach, preach, shepherd, and generally care for all the daily functions in their local churches. Through the power of the Holy Spirit, they were truly self-governing, self-supporting, and self-propagating. They were responsible for the entire church ministry. Except Bible translation!

Since the days of Carey, Judson, and the earliest pioneers in the modern era of missions, Bible translation has predominately been done by individuals from outside the local church. Previously, I had not given the topic much thought. It was just understood by most of us who had been trained to be church planters that Bible translation required specialized training. In November 2014, an event happened in the Himalayan foothills of Nepal that forever changed my thinking about Bible translation and the role of the local church.

Earlier that year, I had started work on the research for my doctoral dissertation. I was focusing on new trends in Bible translation. Some organizations were testing crowd sourced approaches connecting language speakers through the internet to do translation work. WA was working with a group testing computer assisted translation. It was an exciting time seeing new approaches emerging. The big question on everyone's mind was, *what about the quality?* This was also the question on my mind and thus became the focus of my research.

Then MAST (Mobilized Assistance Supporting Translation) happened. WA piloted a new approach to Bible translation in June 2014 with five translation teams representing five different languages from local churches in Nepal. The test was a success and plans were in the works for the next pilot test. One of the first communications I saw regarding the next test said, *a team of 26 translators from the B language in Nepal will translate the New Testament at a two-week workshop this November.* My initial thought was, *this has got to be a typo. There is no way anyone translates the New Testament in two-weeks—not with any level of accuracy.* I went to my friend, Dan Kramer, who created the MAST methodology and asked, "Dan, did I hear correctly? Are you planning a two-week event with the goal of translating an entire New Testament? With 26 people?"

"Yeah, it sounds crazy." He said.

"More like insane!"

He went on, "So, we learned at the June event that translators can produce around 34-35 verses each day. With roughly 7,900 verses in the New Testament, it would take 26 people to translate the New Testament in two weeks."

"Okay, I get the math. But, an entire New Testament? It just sounds — well, crazy! What about the quality?" I asked.

"Great question! We also learned at the June event from the expert consultants participating that the translations using MAST were as good in quality as translations done using traditional methods." He said.

"You know. I'm writing my dissertation on the quality of Bible translations using these new approaches like MAST. Would you mind if I joined the team to document the process and use the findings in my research?"

Dan graciously agreed to have me to join the team in November.

A New Perspective

It was a long travel itinerary with three flights and two long layovers. I don't sleep well on planes and failed to get much of a nap during the layovers. So, from wheels up in Orlando to touch down in Kathmandu, it had been nearly 45 hours since I had slept. After an hour-long car ride out of the city up into the Himalayan foothills, we arrived at the retreat center where we would be staying for the two-week event. As soon as it was appropriate, I went to my room to get some much-needed sleep.

The next day, I woke and joined the group for breakfast. Dan and the team had been hard at work the night before making final arrangements for the start of the workshop. As we ate, Dan mentioned, "I have some good news and some bad news. Which do you want first?"

"Let's get the bad news out of the way first." We responded.

"Alright. So, we were planning on 26 translators to participate in the event. That is what we communicated to the church leaders as the need. It looks like the 13 that showed up are the only ones coming to the event. That being said, it looks like a New Testament in two weeks could be off the table."

"Okay. What's the good news?"

"The good news is that they arrived two days early and we have already wrapped up the preliminary evaluations. So, we can get started on translating today which may put a complete New Testament back on the table!"

From there, we started the day with a time of worship and then jumped right into the workshop. The translators were divided up into four teams based on their skill levels as determined in the evaluations that took place the night before while I was sleeping. WA staff members were assigned to each team as facilitators to assist with explaining the process and answering questions. I spent time with each team as an observer documenting the steps. The first couple of days seemed a bit chaotic, but by the third day everyone had settled into the routine of drafting and checking the translation.

There were multiple checking steps including key word and verse by verse checking. As I documented the steps, I was also trained on the spot to help with the checking. I remember checking the work with one of the translators. She would read a portion of the passage and an interpreter would orally translate it into English for me. We came to a verse that mentioned *evil spirits*. I asked, "Did you use a word from your language for evil spirits or did you use the Nepali word?"

"I used the word from our language." She replied.

"What does that word mean? Describe it to me."

"These are spirit beings." She said.

"Spirits of people who died?"

"No. That would be a different word."

Later in the passage, we again encountered the term *evil spirit*. Only, that time she had used the other word for evil spirit which meant the spirits of family members who had recently died. I suggested that she discuss this with others on her translation team. She did and together they chose to use the word from the previous verse that meant spirit beings and not the spirits of family members who died.

At the end of a full day of drafting and checking, the teams all gathered together in the meeting room after dinner for a public reading of the Scriptures that had been translated that day. The first night as the first team began reading, I looked around the room and saw some of the translators weeping. I leaned over to one of the English-speaking translators sitting next to me and asked, "Why are they crying?" She said, "This is the first time we have heard God's Word read out loud in our language. These are tears of joy." A group conversation followed with everyone from all the teams participating. The person next to me did her best to help me keep up with the conversation. It seemed intense. She said, "They are discussing the use of a certain word in the passage. That gentleman is one of the elders in the church. He is highly respected and he asked why the team chose to use a Nepali word instead of the word from our language."

"What did the team say? Why did they choose to use the Nepali word?" I asked.

"They are saying that they chose the Nepali word because that is the word that everyone will understand. The word that the elder suggested from our language is not used much anymore and not many people will understand."

In the end, the group chose to use the Nepali word as it would be more widely understood. The next evening, one of the pastors led the discussion as the groups worked together to improve their translation.

As I watched those discussions, I couldn't help thinking *we are experiencing modern day Antioch—Paul and Barnabas moments debating the truths of Scripture.* I just smiled as the church leaders and members read and discussed God's Word. They were wrestling with the meaning of the texts and determining the best way to capture the author's intended message in their translation. This had to be what God envisioned when He communicated His intent to make His manifold wisdom known through the church.

By the end of the two weeks, the teams had translated just over half of their New Testament by completing the four gospels and Paul's two letters to Timothy. They left with the Scriptures in their heart language and I left with a new perspective on Bible translation: it can and should be done by the church.

What Did You See?

In the Spring of 2016, I was sitting near the gate for my next flight at the Beijing airport on my way to a translation workshop in Myanmar. It was a long layover and there were only a few other people sitting nearby. Two appeared to be from the US. One spoke to the other, "Are you traveling to Myanmar on business or pleasure?"

"I'm going to visit my son who works for the State Department." She said.

Then he looked at me and said, "You look like you might be going to Myanmar for the same reason I'm going."

"Really? What makes you say that?" I replied.

"I don't know. I just got the feeling you might be headed there for the same reason." I could tell he was purposing to be careful with the conversation. Then he asked, "What do you do for a living?"

"I am the Vice President of Finance for Wycliffe Associates."

"See, I knew we were going to Myanmar for the same reason!" He said.

It was a random meeting, but a welcome connection with a team member as we finished our travels together. I was glad for his company for the remainder of the trip.

I had attended other workshops leading up to this one. So, I had a good understanding of the MAST process and had gained a great deal of confidence in local church leaders ability to do Bible translation. But this workshop was unlike the others I had previously attended as we would be working with 130 believers from a single language group. Our support team also numbered more than any translation team I had worked with in past workshops. It would be a test of my confidence in the process and the ability of the church to do this work.

The first day we divided the group into 27 translation teams assigning a facilitator from WA to each team to provide additional instructions and assist the teams with their questions. This was the first workshop for some of these facilitators. Instead of taking a team myself, I worked with the first-timers to answer their questions and help them when they ran into difficulties on their teams.

By the end of the second day, some of them were approaching me with concerns.

"Tim, you have been to other events. Is this how it is supposed to work?" One asked.

"Actually, each event is slightly different. All of them start out rough like this, but usually by the third or fourth day things settle down."

"I've been a part of Bible translation for years and I am struggling to see how this is going to produce a quality translation." Another commented.

"Well, let's give the process a chance before we come to any conclusions on the quality." I suggested.

In truth, I was having my own doubts at this point in the workshop. Comments from friends back home were coming to mind. *They can't even read! How can they possibly do Bible translation? This work requires rigorous training and experience! There is no way anything done that fast can be good!* That night I couldn't fall asleep, my mind was so full of concerns. But then, as if hearing an audible voice this question came, *what did you see during the quality checking steps?* I thought to myself, *as individuals read their newly translated texts, I saw team members following along in their source text. I saw others on the teams asking questions. I saw pastors and church leaders reviewing and comparing the text with the source*. As I reflected on what I had seen, a sense of peace came over me and I was able to fall asleep.

The next morning, I went to one of the facilitators who had previously been involved in Bible translation and asked if he would be interested in conducting a test with me. While I was at peace with what I had observed in the checking steps, I felt it would be beneficial to spot check the work. His team was average in skills compared to the other teams. So, I thought testing their work would give a reasonable indication of what was taking place around the room. Together, we conducted a more traditional consultant check of a passage his team had completed. It was a narrative passage from the Old Testament. As we listened to the oral back translation we could tell that the content was complete and accurate compared to the Biblical languages text we had in front of us. There was the exception of one phrase—*temple of the Lord* was simply translated *temple*. "Could you read that section again?" I asked. Sure enough, it was simply translated *temple*.

"What does that word temple mean?" I asked.

"It's a place of worship." They said.

"Whose temple is it? Who would you worship in this temple?"

"No one owns it. It's just a place of worship."

"But I'm seeing that this should say *the temple of the Lord*. Why didn't you translate it that way?"

"Our source text doesn't say that. It just says temple."

They were using Judson's translation of the Burmese Bible as their source text because it was the only public domain text available for use at the time. And, their translation was true to the source text, which did not include "of the Lord".

The test revealed a deficiency in the source text, but it confirmed for me the peace I had in the translation process and it strengthened my confidence in the local church's ability to do Bible translation.

Child's Play!

In the four years since MAST emerged in 2014, I have had the privilege of participating in several workshops as a researcher, facilitator, and team leader. I have seen teams translate the Scripture in written and unwritten forms. As quickly as MAST spread among literate groups, it was adapted and has spread among the oral-only and deaf communities. I have been told and for many years, believed it to be true that we needed to teach the illiterate to read and write in order to give them the

Scriptures. It is as if being literate is equated with a higher level of intelligence. While literacy gives communities access to a broader scope of information, it does not mean they were less intelligent prior. A friend from an oral community made this point to a group of us when he asked, "Have you ever memorized Psalm 119?" We all shook our heads, no. "Why not?" He asked.

"Well, it's a very long passage of Scripture." One said.

"I've never even considered it." Came another.

"Child's play!" He said. "Psalm 119 would be nothing for our people! From childhood, we commit to memory hundreds of years of our history. We can name our forefathers back for generations. When an old person dies in our community, we say that we just lost a library." I was thinking to myself, *the best I can do from memory is name my great-grandpa whom I never met and that's only because I saw his name at the top of the family tree in my grandma's Bible.*

As mentioned earlier, each workshop was slightly different. But, they all had some things in common. One common trait that I experienced at the workshops was the work ethic of the translators and their commitment to the task. For me, attending workshops meant I would be working long hours. I still had daily responsibilities as the VP of Finance. The workshop was extra. So, at the end of the day and on breaks, I would do my best to keep up on my other duties. I learned very quickly that I wasn't the only one working late into the night or early hours of the morning at these events. It was common practice for some of the translators to show up to breakfast with another 20-30 verses that they translated the night before. That meant they continued working after the community checking session that ended at nine or ten the night before.

Another common trait that I saw at the workshops was the care that the translators had for quality. I remember commenting to a local leader, "It is refreshing to see these guys paying attention to the details. You can tell they want a quality translation."

"That's no surprise. When they take their translation home, they know that the pastors will compare their work to the common language Bibles they use for preaching." He said.

"So, when the pastors preach from the common language Bibles, aren't they translating Scripture as they go?"

"Yes, that is the only way their congregations get to hear God's Word—until now. Now they will hear it read in their own language!"

"Wouldn't they value the checking efforts of the group here and see the translation as an improvement over a single person translating on the spot?"

"Sure, they will! But, they will still compare the translation to be sure it says the same thing as the common language Bible."

I have learned much since my first MAST workshop and anticipate learning many more things in the days ahead. Of the things I've learned, the most important is that the local church—anywhere in the world—can do Bible translation. And they can do it well! It should not have been a surprise to me. I had been trained and fully believed that local churches and church leaders could self-govern, self-support, and self-propagate. It wasn't much of a step for me to accept that they could also self-manage Bible translation.

Since that first workshop, WA has helped over 1,000 language groups get started with their Scripture translation projects using MAST— not doing Bible translation for them, but rather, teaching and empowering them as churches and church leaders to do Bible translation for themselves—now and for future generations! I can't help thinking now that this is part of God's intent in making His manifold wisdom known through the Church.

Prayer

Lord, thank you for showing me that an empowered church can do many things—even Bible translation.

Lord, use me and others to empower churches everywhere to do Bible translation now and for future generations.

Chapter Eleven

All Things

Verse

And we know that all things work together
for good to them that love God...
Romans 8:28 KJV

Introduction

"Son, I have something important I need to ask you." These were Dad's opening words to a conversation I will never forget. We were sitting in his car outside my house at the end of our weekend together. I was thirteen and thought, *this must be big if Dad is asking me for my opinion.*

"Yeah, no problem. How can I help?" I said.

"Son, you know how much I love you. Right?" He asked.

"Sure, dad."

"You know how much I love my job." He said.

"Of course." I replied.

"Well, a good friend of mine has offered me the sales managers job at his dealership."

"Dad! That's great!" I exclaimed.

"Son, here's the thing that I need to ask you. His dealership is in Tennessee. Would you be okay if Shirley, me and the girls move to Tennessee?" Shirley was my step-mom who had three daughters from a previous marriage.

"Oh! Well..." Before I could get the words out, Dad quickly continued.

"I know we wouldn't be able to be together on weekends. But you could come down for a month or more in the summer. It would really be good for the family. What do you think?"

I swallowed hard and said, "If you think this is best, then I guess you need to do it."

"So, you're okay with us moving?" He asked again.

"Sure, if that's what you think is best." I replied. Then I got out of the car and waved as he drove off. I was overcome with emotions as I walked into the house where my mom and my new step-dad, Bill, were waiting for me. The ache was deep, deeper than anything I remember feeling before and I wept for a long time. Questions flooded my mind. *Why God? Why is this happening? How can this possibly be good for the family?*

It took time. But the ache eventually subsided and the empty spot that dad's decision left in my life was soon filled by two amazing men who became my fathers, Bill Irwin and Neal Raetz.

Bill and my mom met when I was eleven. Mom was waiting tables at a pub. Bill came in one night with his brother Tom and cousin John. They happened to sit in Mom's section. I can still hear John describe the night. "Yeah, Bill was taken with your mom. She was playing hard to get. We told her, 'If you don't agree to go out with him, we'll wreck the joint!'" Bill was a 6'2", 230-pound guy who played offensive line in college football. So, they probably could have "wrecked the joint" if they chose. John likely embellished things a bit, but it made for a great story. And, it still makes me laugh every time I think about it.

In just a few weeks, Bill and my mom got married. I was happy for mom and deep down, I was also happy for me and Mark, my little brother. Bill was a great step-dad—a gentle giant who treated us like his own boys. He owned a radiator repair shop and could fix or build about anything he put his mind to. While I never did learn how to lay a decent bead of solder, Bill did teach me to work with my hands—swinging a hammer and turning wrenches. He had some fun sayings like, "Fool me once shame on you, fool me twice shame on me." And, he always had words of wisdom when I needed them.

Neal became part of my life when I started dating his daughter Nancy. I was fifteen when we met and wanted to make a good impression on Neal. In one of our early conversations, I remember telling him, "Mr. Raetz, when it comes to guy/girl things, you've got nothing to worry about."

"Yeah, actually I do!" He said, setting the tone for real, open and honest conversations. I didn't know it then, but Neal would become one of my best friends in life. As we began to get to know each other, he purchased a set of golf clubs and joined me on the golf course. Later, I found out that fishing was his preferred outdoor activity. So, I accumulated fishing equipment and spent time with him fishing.

From those days of dating till today, Neal has taught me so much—sometimes he even uses words. I remember learning how to treat Nancy like a lady simply by watching how he took care of Nancy's mom, Carol. He would open doors for her, speak respectfully to her, and always kiss her when leaving the house. As I spent more time with the family, he took the opportunity to mentor me in finances, teaching me how to budget. More importantly, he would regularly ask, "So, how is your walk with the Lord? Are you spending time reading your Bible and praying?" I turned 50 this year and he still asks me those questions.

The pain of losing the closeness with my own dad was beyond words. When I could not see the good in my situation, God stepped in through Bill and Neal and began showing me how He can make "…all things work together for good…" even things that hurt—things that didn't make sense to me.

Broken Bones

"Mr. Neu, this is Brown's Gymnastics" a woman's voice responded as I answered the phone. Brown's was where Sarah worked as a gymnastics instructor when she was a teenager.

"Hi! What can I do for you?" I asked.

"Your daughter, Sarah, hurt her arm while working out. It would be good if you could come to the gym." She said.

"Sure, I'm actually only a couple of blocks away. I'll be right there." I was already on my way to the gym to pick Sarah up from work when I got the call.

As I turned the corner, I could see emergency vehicles in the parking lot at the gym. I remember thinking, *please don't let that be for Sarah.* My heart was pounding hard as I entered the building. I could see a couple of first responders huddled over Sarah as a third approached me.

"Are you Sarah's dad?" He asked.

"Yes, I am."

"Sir, we are working to stabilize your daughter's arm. We would like to give her morphine to ease the pain."

"Absolutely! Whatever you need to do!" I said as I got close enough to see what was going on. It was bad! Arms are not meant to bend that way! Both bones were broken! My little girl was in so much pain, the morphine didn't even help.

The next 18 hours were agonizing as the hospital staff attempted to manage the pain while we waited on the surgeon to arrive. Every muscle twitch was torture for Sarah. Nancy and I felt helpless as Sarah cried out in pain. I prayed, "God, please take the pain away." He didn't—it continued for hours as none of the pain medications seemed to help.

The team finally arrived to take Sarah into surgery. I remember the anesthesiologist asking, "How long has she been suffering like this?"

"Going on 18 hours now." I replied.

He was visibly irritated that she had been allowed to be in pain for so long and said, "Well, we are going to deal with that right now!" He quickly injected medication into the IV tubing and Sarah was asleep in seconds.

"Where were you 18 hours ago?" I asked. He just shook his head as the team wheeled her into surgery.

Two titanium plates and twelve screws later, Sarah was awake and smiling. She still hurt, but nothing like the hours before the surgery. While she was in the operating room, my cell phone rang. It was Jeff, Sarah's boyfriend in Kansas.

"Hey, Jeff."

"Hi, Mr. Neu. How's Sarah doing?" He asked.

"Well, they finally took her in for surgery." I said.

"I'm really concerned for her. Would it be okay if I flew down to be with her?" He asked.

I don't recall exactly how I replied. But, I remember thinking, *this is really not a good time for a visit. Then again, Jeff visiting would definitely make Sarah happy.*

Whatever I said, Jeff was on the next plane to Orlando. We didn't tell Sarah he was coming. So, when he walked in the room, she was ecstatic! His presence was better than the medicine she was taking for the pain. While we were feeling helpless just hours earlier, God was working good through this experience to draw Jeff and Sarah closer together in their relationship. They got married a couple of years later. And this hospital experience was only the beginning for them as a couple as Sarah has had several health challenges over the years. Jeff has been there providing the love and care she needs.

When in the middle of a crisis, it is not easy to see how God can work all things for good. Broken bones literally hurt! Relief from pain is the only good thing you want in that moment. But, God seems to do more good than what we imagine or ask. From the broken bones and other health challenges, I have seen Jeff and Sarah bless others with care and compassion that only comes through personal experiences.

Crisis of Faith

Nancy and I chose to home school our girls through junior high and high school. This approach seemed to work well for Sarah as she had her sights set on getting married and being a mom. Stephanie had her sights set on college and career. So, as she approached high school, we began to re-evaluate her schooling options.

We had not considered public schools up to that point in time. The worldview taught in public schools conflicts with our Christian world view and it didn't seem fitting to subject our girls to the contrary teaching or environment. However, our opinion began to change as we heard positive reports about one of the local high schools. It was a technology magnet school with a student population of roughly 500. As a magnet school, students were taught specific skills in computer programing, networking, or graphic design. It reminded me of the vocational schools we used to have when I was a teenager. If students applied themselves, they could graduate with tech certifications and college credits—a full year's worth.

Stephanie excelled with technology. So, we visited the school to learn more about the program and the environment. The experience went well and we left the school feeling positive about the opportunity. In addition, Stephanie had shown a great deal of Spiritual growth through her junior high years. She was disciplined in her Scripture reading and prayer life. The group of kids she spent time with were reading Lee Strobel's books and attending his conferences. We thought, *maybe this could be a good thing for Steph*.

We filled out the paperwork for registration and Stephanie began classes at the public school as a freshman. The first year seemed to go well. As expected, Steph excelled in her classes. In fact, she participated in a science competition with three other classmates that took first place in the school. They were one of four teams selected to present their project in Washington DC. It was quite an accomplishment.

As the second year began, we noticed some subtle changes. Steph spent more and more time with her non-Christian friends at school and less time with her Christian friends. We expected some changes, but didn't realize how significant the changes were until Steph came to us one evening.

"Mom, Dad—I have something important I need to say to you guys."

"Okay." We said as we sat down together in our living room.

"I have given this a lot of thought. And it is probably going to be a shock to you." She said.

"What is it? You're starting to worry me." I said.

"My friends all have different views on faith. And, they all live good lives. I know this is going to be hard for you to hear. But, I just don't believe what you believe anymore. I don't believe there is a God. And, I don't want to live by the same rules anymore."

She was right! We were in shock! One thing we learned with Steph was that once she thought something through and made up her mind, there was little chance of changing it.

We were clearly in crisis mode as a family at this point. The weeks and months that followed were miserable. It seemed like the more we tried to talk and reason with Steph the further apart we got. I remember bouncing from emotion to emotion—anger, sorrow, guilt, and frustration. Questions flooded my mind. *How did this happen? Why didn't I see it coming sooner? What was I thinking sending her to the public school? When am I going to wake up from this nightmare?* I remember feeling hurt and rejected. The ache was intense and deep—deeper then what I felt as a teen when my dad moved to Tennessee. I felt like I failed at the most important job God gave me as a dad. Friends and family did their best to comfort and counsel me. *This isn't about you! This is about Steph! You can't take this personally!* My pastor encouraged me to read the Psalms. I tried. But I didn't find comfort—only more sorrow.

Then one day, months after Steph's announcement, words came to me that I had shared with the teens in Sunday school, *study God's word and develop your own convictions. Don't rent or borrow truth from others. Make it your own and stand firm in your faith.* Easy words to say especially when our kids are making God-honoring choices. Not easy to accept when they conclude things differently from us. It struck me that this was Steph's moment. Whether she stands or falls, the decision is hers.

From that point on, Nancy and I did everything we could to support and love Stephanie no matter what she decided. For the next seven years, we prayed and waited for God to do something to restore her faith.

While it felt like a long time to wait, God did work in Stephanie's life primarily through a relationship with a young man she met at work, Sam. He had recently graduated from college with a degree in pastoral ministry. As they spent time together discussing life and faith, Stephanie began rediscovering her faith. It didn't happen overnight, but we watched and continued to pray. And God faithfully worked to draw her back to Himself. In time, Sam and Stephanie would marry and serve the Lord in full-time ministry with us at Wycliffe Associates.

Through Stephanie's crisis in faith, I learned how God can take the deepest hurt in my life and work it for His good. It took years! But, God allowed me to see Stephanie reclaim her faith — not my faith — not anyone else's faith — her faith! And that's the good that God worked!

Was This Necessary?

On the Friday before Mother's Day, 2018, I shut down my computer an hour early. The weather was perfect for flying. My brother-in-law had lent me his Cessna 172 and my son-in-law had been giving me flying lessons. I had soloed a couple weeks earlier and I planned to fit a student solo flight in before dark. On the way to my car, I felt my phone vibrate. So, I checked the message before pulling out of the parking lot. It was a text from Nancy. "Heading to Neumours to meet Sarah. Kate's blood sugar was 500." Kate is our three-year-old granddaughter and Neumours is the local children's hospital.

I quickly called, "What's going on? Your text said Kate's blood sugar was 500!"

"Yes, 500! Sarah said that Kate had been drinking lots of water the last few days and started having wetting accidents. Amazingly, she thought to check Kate's blood sugar." She explained.

"Wow! Okay! You're headed to the ER?" I asked.

"Yes, I'm on my way there now."

"All right. I'll be there shortly." I said.

I diverted to the hospital to join Sarah, Kate, and Nancy in the ER as thoughts of perfect weather and solo flights were suddenly gone. When I walked into the room, I gave Sarah a hug. She was doing her best to hold back the tears as she already knew that Kate's life had forever changed. Nancy said, "The doctor has confirmed that it's Type 1 Diabetes." I looked down at Kate.

"Hi Grandpa." She said.

"Hey, Katy-K. How are you doing?" I asked.

"Look at my stickers." She said as she pointed to the places where the sensors were attached to her little body. Then she held up her finger and said, "Look, Grandpa! My finger is red!" The oxygen sensor lit up the end of her finger.

"Wow. Look at those stickers and look at your finger. That's so cool!"

Looking at Kate, you wouldn't have guessed that anything was wrong. She appeared perfectly normal and seemed to be enjoying the extra attention she was getting from everyone. Well, most of the attention! She didn't like the finger stick to test her blood—not at all! Little did she know at the time, but finger sticks and insulin injections were going to be part of her daily routine moving forward. For the moment, Grandpa and Kate leaned back and watched her favorite Disney movie, *Moana*. The next couple of hours, life was good. After that, the work began for Sarah and Jeff as they were instantly thrust into a new way of life—caring for a three-year-old with Type 1 diabetes.

At age 50, I still ask God, *Why? Was this necessary?* In theory and through experiences like rejection, broken bones, and broken relationships, I have seen God work things "together for good". *But, why Kate? And, what good can He work in this?* The truth is that I don't know why He allowed this for Kate. And, I don't know the good He will work. Paul said, "…we know that all things work together for good to them that love God…" It may take years before we see the good God works in Kate's life. Just like it took years to see the good God worked in Stephanie's life.

Prayer

God, thank you for working all things together for good—even the things I can't understand.

God, help me patiently anticipate the good you will work—even when I can see no possible good.

Chapter Twelve

A Sense of Urgency

Verse

Redeeming the time, because the days are evil. Ephesians 5:16 KJV

Introduction

"You can only spend it once." My boss often uses this phrase with the leadership team as we begin working on the budget for the coming fiscal year. It is his way of reminding us that our spending decisions matter and that we need to be strategic with the funds we've been given to manage.

Time is equally important and how we choose to use it also matters. Paul told the believers at Ephesus, "Redeem the time..." The first time this thought came into focus for me was in my junior year of high school. I was a captain on the varsity soccer team and that year one of the cheerleaders died with her parents in a plane crash. The news was shocking. Our team gathered at the assistant coach's house for a time of reflection. I shared a brief devotional attempting to encourage my teammates in our hope of heaven. But, I remember thinking, *man, life is so fragile and short—there are no guarantees of tomorrow*. For a time, I think we all lived with a little more purpose and urgency.

I remember another "redeeming the time" moment much later in a hospital in Hudson, FL, with my mom's family. My Papa had been battling an acute type of leukemia and was in bad shape. Only two visitors were allowed in his room at a time. It was my turn. My uncle's wife, Cathy, went in with me. It was tough seeing him in that condition. I heard what seemed like a soft voice in my ear saying, *time is short here—talk about the hope of heaven one more time.* I took his hand and said, "Papa, it's me, Tim. I don't know if you can hear me. Just want to say how much I love you. Do you remember our talks about Jesus? Before you go, I want you to know that He loves you too." At that point, I shared the gospel of salvation not so much for my Papa, as for Cathy. As it turned out, it was the last time I saw my Papa and the last time I had an opportunity to speak with Cathy about salvation as she and my uncle separated in the months that followed.

Not all situations in life are necessarily as urgent as that visit to the hospital, but the admonition from Paul seems to indicate that we need to live life with a sense of urgency to redeem the time.

Timely, Relevant Information

When I accepted the Vice President of Finance position with WA, the finance team was a hard-working group of people fully dedicated to their respective tasks. At the time, management's expectation was for the team to close a month within eight working days of the new month and close the fiscal year within thirty-five working days of the new year. The first time I saw these performance goals, I thought *surely it doesn't take that long to close a month or year-end.*

With prior experience reducing month-end closing processes from days to hours at NTM, it was time to review and evaluate the activities to find efficiencies. It didn't take long for me to see that the team had been conditioned to focus on details that created tons of work producing very little in terms of benefit. I remember sitting with one staff member to observe her processes and noticed that she was painstakingly comparing vendor mailing addresses on invoices with those in our computer system. I asked, "Is this what you do with every invoice from every vendor? Even our regular vendors?"

"Yes, we want to be sure to send checks to the right address." She said.

"That's good! We certainly wouldn't want to send checks to the wrong address. Have you made any address changes recently?"

"Not recently, but we catch lots of mistakes and make lots of changes."

"Really? Well, how many changes have you made in the last quarter?"

"None."

"How about in the last six months or year?"

"I don't actually know. Maybe one or two."

Next, she printed the checks and started for the door to deliver them to the first signer. I ask, "What about the invoices? Do you not include the supporting documentation with the checks for the signers to review?" I was surprised to learn that the checks were being signed without the supporting documentation. This was an example of working hard prioritizing minor things and skipping major steps that could have allowed for the mishandling of WA's funds. We immediately changed the procedures to include sound internal controls.

After reviewing all the processes and procedures, I gathered the team together for a meeting. I thanked everyone for their help and then said, "We have a number of opportunities to gain efficiencies. Over the next few months, we are going to reduce the time it takes to close the month. In fact, my goal is to get our timeline down from eight to two days by the end of this fiscal year."

"It has been work getting things done in the eight days. How are we going to get it down to two?" One brave team member voiced what most of them were thinking.

"Great question. For starters, we are going to begin processing work as we receive it. Contribution batches need to be processed and posted daily. Vendor payments need to be processed daily instead of weekly." I said.

"What's wrong with the way we've been doing things?"

"That's a fair question. Nothing is technically wrong. But, my primary concern is that our managers have been making decisions with out-of-date information."

"Oh—well, the mangers don't read the financial reports anyway."

"Precisely my point! The information in our reports is irrelevant by the time the managers receive them. We have already processed another eight to ten days of data by the time they get our reports."

In that conversation and the ones that followed, I was able cast a vision of urgency in providing timely, relevant information so that managers could make informed decisions. With advancements in technology, we implemented changes that gave managers real-time access to financial information enabling them to move initiatives forward with confidence.

Uncommon Practice

In the last thirty years, I have been privileged to work with teams that caught a vision for working with a sense of urgency, redeeming time. We gained efficiencies reducing days of work to hours. In fact, my current team has achieved a level of efficiency that produces month end reports to upper management by 8:00 AM on the first working day of the new month.

This level of performance in accounting and finance is not common—at least not in my circles of connection. On occasion, I have talked about our efforts with peers at round table discussions. Following one round table, a friend of mine from another organization asked me to speak at a conference for financial professionals. It was intimidating to think of addressing a larger group of my peers, but I accepted the invitation. My presentation focused on the need as financial staff to provide timely, relevant information to decision makers. I remember sharing my team's story and our pursuit of same day processing so that we could provide real time information to managers. At that time, we were still taking one or two days to close a month before providing management with reports.

After the presentation, we had a question and answer time. I prefer the questions in advance so that I can give thought to my answers. But that wasn't going to happen in this setting. I had to go with the questions as asked. The first question came, "How do you handle things like bank fees and interest?"

"Great question. We use our online banking portal to get the information as quickly as possible. If the needed information is not readily available, we use estimates for the management reports. Fees and interest are easy to predict. Estimates are close enough to the actual numbers for managers to make informed decisions."

The follow up question was, "Doesn't that conflict with accounting and reporting standards?"

"It could if we were talking about audited financial statements. We do wait on final numbers to be published by the bank before we close out our year end."

The next question, "With the speed, are you finding the team making mistakes? Do you have an increased number of correcting entries?"

"Another great question. Yes, we do make mistakes and we are making correcting entries. Are we experiencing more mistakes than before? Not really. In fact, now that managers are looking at their reports more often, we are catching things that were being completely overlooked in the past."

The rest of the questions seemed to be focused on poking holes in the process, citing reporting standards, or making statements of how this approach was flawed and could never work in their situation. It was as if the focus on precision in following reporting standards would produce perfect reports for managers, even though we all had experienced otherwise. It was discouraging as a presenter because I felt like the group missed the point that timely, relevant financial information empowers decision makers to more effectively accomplish the organization's mission.

As an accounting professional, I clearly have the expertise to produce financial statements with precision. But, I wanted more. I wanted to empower our management teams with the information they needed to accomplish our mission. In working with my team to empower managers, we ended up gaining their help in reviewing and improving the quality of our work. The managers were the experts when it came to the spending details for their departments and projects. With their eyes regularly looking at the reports, we were getting questions about details that in the past had never been asked. It exposed items posted to wrong departments or detailed expense accounts. Before the changes, these types of mistakes went undetected.

So, we had been producing financial statements in the past that fully complied with accounting and reporting standards—technically correct in every way. But, the detailed reports for our managers suffered. By working with a sense of urgency and redeeming the time in accounting, not only did the managers help us keep the information more accurate, they were empowered to make better-informed spending decisions. As a result, our managers could also redeem the time by responding more quickly to the needs of Bible translation teams around the world giving even more language groups access to God's Word.

We Can Do Better

As part of the research for my dissertation, I traveled and interviewed people involved in translation from various organizations. I wanted to gain a better understanding of the commonly accepted approach in Bible translation. While traveling in India, I had the opportunity to visit with a team that had been working on their New Testament for several years. They were on pace to complete the translation in approximately eight years. That was considered a good pace as New Testaments had at one time been taking thirty or more years to complete.

After introductions, I asked, "Who does the quality checking for your work?"

The team leader spoke up, "We check each other's work as we go, but the final checking is done by an expert consultant."

"So, your team does checking. What training have they had?"

"Well, everyone has at least a bachelor's degree in Bible or theology. Some have their master's degree and I am working on my doctorate."

"That's great! The expert consultant that you mentioned, where is he from?"

"He's from another country."

"Oh. How often does he come to check your work and what does he do differently?"

"He travels here once or sometimes twice a year and he goes through the same checking steps that we use."

"Really? The same steps?

"Yes, the exact same steps."

"What happens with the Scriptures while you wait for him to come and check it? Are the passages you've completed being made available to pastors or churches for use?"

"The Scripture sit right over there until they can be checked by the consultant." He was pointing to the bookshelf behind him. I was thinking, *these guys have all the training required to be consultants and more importantly they know the language and culture, but their work sits on a shelf!*

"One more question. Have you considered making these available sooner?"

"Yes, but if we do, we will lose funding from our sponsoring organization. They require an expert consultant check before we publish the Scriptures for use."

You've got to be kidding me! We can do better than this, was the first thought that went through my mind. The next was, *this situation totally correlates with my experiences in finance. Redeeming the time as a finance guy directly impacted the work of Bible translation. How much more impact would this principle have in this community if these brothers were empowered to redeem the time with their translations?*

It's Too Fast!

Time is important. We have no idea how many days God has given us to do His work. How we use the time we've been given matters. Paul said to redeem the time which communicates to me living with a sense of urgency even with everyday tasks like accounting. While misunderstood by peers, my sense of urgency working with accounting teams was worth the effort.

A young man in Nepal working with another Bible translation organization was struggling with a similar thought regarding urgency. He was not content with the status quo. Bible translation was taking too long for his people. So, he asked Dan Kramer, a friend and colleague, "Will you help us develop a new way to do Bible translation? Something that will speed up the work." What Dan and his team came up with was amazing! At my first workshop, I witnessed thirteen believers in that two-week event do for Bible translation what I had been doing with my finance teams. They accelerated Bible translation by adding the quality checking steps right into the translation process. Just like providing timely financial information helped managers to make better decisions, timely quality checking helped the translators make better decisions with their Scriptures. It was brilliant! When we asked, "Why did you use that word?" They had an immediate, intelligent response because they had just translated the passage. It resulted in a greatly reduced time line—from decades and years to months and weeks.

Later, when people questioned the quality because of the speed, I was reminded of the times my peers questioned the quality of our management reports. They would say, "It's too fast! You probably made a bunch of mistakes!" The truth is that timely information empowered our managers to participate in checking the financial data for accuracy. I saw the same thing happening at the workshops. Translated Scriptures were being quality checked the same day they are translated instead of months after the fact. These translators, experts in their own language, gave timely input during the quality checking that improved the accuracy of their Scriptures.

What I witnessed in the two-week workshop—nearly 50% of the New Testament translated—was nothing short of miraculous. These believers clearly worked with a sense of urgency and demonstrated to me and the world the ultimate effort in redeeming the time.

Prayer

Lord, give me a sense of urgency every day so that I redeem the time.

Lord, show me how to encourage others to live with that same sense of urgency so that they too redeem the time.

Chapter Thirteen

Scriptures Make a Difference

Verse

…crave pure spiritual milk, so that by it you may grow up in your salvation, now that you have tasted that the Lord is good.
1 Peter 2:2-3

Introduction

Sunday afternoons at Grandma and Papa's was something I looked forward to as a little boy. Grandma always had an amazing meal for us—fried chicken, green beans, slaw, biscuits, and a huge bowl of banana pudding. The banana pudding was my favorite! Those vanilla wafers and the meringue topping made it tough to stop with one serving. Many Sundays I would lay on the living room floor after lunch and fall asleep watching golf, not because I loved watching golf, but because I was too full to move.

Occasionally, my Papa would say, "How about some homemade?"

"Homemade! Yeah, I want homemade!" Homemade ice cream was the best.

"Who's going to help me crank?" He'd ask.

"Me! Let me crank, Papa!" I loved helping Papa crank the ice cream maker. "Papa! Check! I think it's ready!"

"Oh, come on now. It can't be ready yet. You haven't been cranking that long."

"I know, but it is starting to get thick. I can feel it when I crank."

And so, it would go as we took turns cranking the ice cream until it was ready. It was exciting doing things with Papa. He made everything fun. If he liked something, then I liked it too—tomatoes, cucumbers, green onions, strawberry short cake, and corn bread immediately come to mind.

But there was one thing he loved that I never did like—buttermilk! I remember my first (and last!) experience tasting buttermilk. "Mmm! This is so good! You should try some." Papa said as I was watching him drink a big glass of buttermilk and snack on some green onions.

"Yeah! I'll have a glass." I said.

"Now Ken! You shouldn't do that to him!" Grandma said to Papa.

"You don't know. He might like it." Papa responded.

"Yeah, I might like it." I said.

"Okay. But don't say I didn't warn you!" She said as she poured me a small glass.

I loved drinking milk. So, I took a big mouth full just like I would a normal glass of milk. It was a good thing I was close to the sink because it came out of my mouth as fast as it went in. It was the nastiest thing I had ever tasted. Once I caught my breath and rinsed the taste out of my mouth, I said, "Papa, why do you like drinking that stuff? It's nasty!"

When he stopped laughing, he asked me, "Why do you like eating grandma's banana pudding?" And, he was serious.

I never really understood how Papa could possibly like the taste of buttermilk. But, he did! He would drink big glasses with different snacks. When we had corn bread, he would crumble a piece up and mix it in his glass of buttermilk. It was something he craved. While the thought of taking another drink of buttermilk myself still makes me shudder, I could relate to the joy Papa got with each swallow as I thought of the things I craved like banana pudding or homemade ice cream.

That experience with my Papa helped me appreciate the fact that people might like and crave different things from what I like and crave. It also prepared me to hear and understand Peter's words, "...crave pure spiritual milk [of the Word] ...". Peter seems to be saying that we should crave God's Word just like Papa craved his buttermilk, or, like I craved banana pudding—enough to eat seconds or thirds until I was too full to move.

Chapters 2000

In the months leading up to the year 2000, some were predicting major chaos with the failure of power grids and the collapse of financial institutions. The pending chaos commonly referred to as Y2K was attributed to the use of a two-digit year field in critical software programs.

Failure to use a four-digit year field in these programs could instantly cripple society and invoke chaos the likes of which we had never seen as soon as the clock struck mid-night on December 31, 1999. Family members and friends were preparing for the worst-case scenario. People were purchasing whole house generators and stocking food pantries with canned goods, anticipating the worst.

I was on the leadership team at NTM's headquarters at the time. As an organization, we had worked through the necessary adjustments in our mission critical software programs expanding the year field from two-digits to four-digits in preparation for Y2K. Being involved with finances, people often asked, "Tim, what do you think about Y2K? Are you concerned?" To which I responded, "No, I'm not concerned. People are making way too much money. They aren't going to let a two-digit year field interrupt their cash flow."

At church, we were preparing for Y2K in a completely different way. While the world was taking precautions and preparing for the chaos, our pastor was introducing a Scripture reading program for the new year to our church. He called it Chapters 2000. He introduced the program one Sunday morning by holding up a signup sheet as he said, "In an effort to encourage each other as a church family, I'm challenging each of you to commit to reading a certain number of chapters each week in your Bibles. Give it some thought and prayer this week. Next week, I will post this signup sheet in the foyer for you to signup stating how many chapters you will read each week for the year. Then, each week after that, you will enter the number of chapters you read the previous week."

On the way home from church Nancy asked, "What did you think about Pastor's Chapters 2000 idea?"

Well, I wasn't ready to comment. So, I answered, "What did you think?"

"I love it!" She said.

"Really? So, what do you love about it?" I asked.

"I love that we are being encouraged to read the Bible. And, I love that we are being encouraged to help each other be successful by showing our progress each week." She said.

"So, you don't find it intrusive to sign in each week with the chapters you've read?"

"No! Why would I? What does it matter anyway? The point is to be reading God's Word regularly. And that is a good thing!"

Of course, she was right! This was about encouraging each other to regularly read God's Word.

The next Sunday, folks were huddled around the signup sheet putting down the number of chapters in God's Word that they were committing to read each week. I eventually made my way over to the signup sheet to log my reading commitment. Looking at the sheet, I saw some big numbers. I remember thinking, *looks like folks are serious about their reading commitment.*

At first, I found myself reading random chapters mostly out of obligation so that I could put the number on the board at church. In time, I took a more purposeful approach to my reading by working through Biblical history in the Old Testament. At some point, it became an obsession instead of an obligation. There were days that I couldn't wait to wrap up the day's work so that I could get home and finish reading the section that I started reading the night before. The more I read, the more I wanted to read.

I remember reading the account of Israel's exodus from Egypt. When Pharaoh finally let the people of Israel go, the passage said, "God did not lead them on the road through the Philistine country, though it was shorter. For God said, 'If they face war, they might change their minds and return to Egypt.'" At the time I thought, *God miraculously delivered them from years of slavery and He was visibly leading them. They had everything they needed to succeed on their journey. How could they possibly change their minds and go back?* Then it dawned on me that the Israelites were armed for battle, but they were not ready for battle. God would need to lead them on a longer, more difficult path to prepare them for the intense battles they would face along the way.

While I had not been asked to walk the same difficult path as the Israelites, I could see from that historical event how God uses difficulties in life to prepare us for His purposes. In moments like that, I learned and experienced what Peter meant when he said, "...crave pure spiritual milk [of the Word], so that by it you may grow...".

Lost Appetite

"It's cancer." Were the words from Ron, a close friend and coworker of mine, in the finance office at NTM.

"What's the prognosis?" I asked.

"The doctor said they caught it early. So, I should be okay after surgery and treatment." He said.

"Sounds hopeful. But, how are you doing?" At that point, there were no more words. Only tears. I put my arm around him and motioned for others close by in the office to join me as we prayed together.

It was a tough season for Ron and his family. He would undergo surgery to remove the cancer followed by radiation and chemo therapy. The hospital was only a couple of miles from the NTM office. I joined the family on the day of the surgery and stopped by to visit every day until he was able to go home. The surgery was a success, but because it was esophageal cancer Ron would need a feeding tube for several weeks. When it was time to remove the feeding tube and return to normal eating, I asked Ron, "So, what are you going to eat first? Are you going to go out and order your favorite meal?"

"Well, I don't know. I mean I haven't felt hungry for a long time." He said.

"You don't feel hungry?"

"No. I lost my appetite several weeks ago." He replied.

"So, there's nothing you're craving after all that time?"

"No-nothing." He said.

"Is that normal?"

"Yeah, the doctors said that I would stop feeling hungry after a few days with the feeding tube. But, they say it will eventually come back once I start eating normally again." He said.

I couldn't imagine not feeling hunger or craving food. It was tough relating to what Ron had described. Then I thought, *this is exactly what happens to me spiritually when I'm not regularly reading God's Word.* I have experienced some amazing seasons of craving God's Word like I did as a kid with the Children's Bible or during Chapters 2000. But, I have sadly also experienced seasons where I couldn't remember the last time I sat down to read a full passage of Scripture—and worse than that didn't even miss it.

Ron's appetite eventually returned just as the doctors said. His body recovered from not eating in the conventional way. The feeding tube sustained him, but it was nothing like the normal body function of savoring and swallowing his favorite foods. The correlation between Ron's physical experience and my spiritual life was so obvious. Too often I had functioned spiritually like I was on a feeding tube—settling for a weekly sermon or Sunday school lesson.

This is likely why Peter gave the instruction to "crave" God's Word. He knew we would have the tendency to neglect it and lose our appetite.

The good news is that the appetite will return just the same as Ron's appetite for food returned. We just need to pick up His Word and read it.

I Want to Do More

With three days left at the two-week MAST event in Nepal, one of the translation teams had completed drafting and checking the gospel of Mark. While the other teams were working to finish translating the other three gospels, a young lady from the team that had just finished Mark said, "What's next? I want to do more!"

The event leaders said, "How about 1 Timothy? Get started with that and see how far your team can get."

"Thank you!" She said and off she went with her team to start work on 1 Timothy. By the end of the day, she was back requesting more. Her team ended up completing both of Paul's letters to Timothy in just two days.

It was an amazing thing to witness. This young lady arrived with the others at this translation workshop not really knowing what to expect. When we told them at the beginning of the workshop that they would be translating God's Word, they all said, "No way! We can't translate God's Word!" But, by the end of the workshop, they had translated nearly half of the New Testament. They had caught on to the work with MAST and the just-in-time training. The more translating they did, the more they wanted to do!

As mentioned previously, I left this workshop with a completely different view of Bible translation. Not only did I see that ordinary people from the local church could do Bible translation, I saw how their first-hand exposure to God's Word in their language instantly impacted their lives. In their checking sessions, they discussed deeper issues in the Scripture. In one of the sessions, as they worked on John 1:14, the question was asked, "What does it mean when it says, 'The Word became flesh'?"

"What came to your mind when you read the verse?" We asked.

"He became a human." One said.

"Do you have a word for that in your language?" We asked.

"Yes, but we were not sure we could use it. Could we say, 'The Word became a human being?"

"We think that would be appropriate. What does the rest of the group think?" We replied.

Everyone was involved in the conversation and they all agreed that this would be the best way to translate "The Word became flesh".

At the end of the workshop, the translation team left with Scriptures in their own language—not yet perfect, but ready for checking and use in their community. Rather than sitting on bookshelves waiting for experts to arrive for checking as I had witnessed in other places, these Scriptures had already been in use and made a difference in the lives of these church members who did the translating. Very soon, these Scriptures would be making a difference back home when the rest of the church joined in the checking effort.

It was easy to see at the workshop how the group grew in their understanding of God's Word. The added blessing was seeing them want more! It was just like Peter had said, "…crave pure spiritual milk [of the Word], so that by it you may grow up…". I remember thinking, *this is it! This is how God is going to spread His Word among the remaining languages of the world still without Scriptures.*

This Is Reformational!

I couldn't wait to share what I saw at the workshop in Nepal with friends and family back home. It had to be one of the most significant events in recent history. My sense was that I had witnessed something that everyone would eventually wish they could have seen for themselves. As I shared my story, I was surprised by the majority of responses. It was completely the opposite of what I expected. Some commented, "MAST is too fast!"

"There is no way the translations can be accurate!"

"Untrained people cannot do Bible translation!"

"You should do more testing!"

"What do the other translation organizations think? If they don't approve it, we won't accept it!"

"It's irresponsible to hand out translations before they have been thoroughly checked."

I was so disappointed. After all, I saw what I saw! A miracle did happen! We personally checked passages and found that the translation was faithful to the source text! Both expert consultants who had participated in the workshop told me, "This translation is on par with those done by trained translators." One recounted, "In 45 verses of checking, we only suggested one edit and that was to add a quotation mark."

As I encountered the negative feedback, I decided to look at how Bible translation had been done in times past. I wanted to know who did Bible translation and more importantly who checked the translation's accuracy. Solomon's words, "there's nothing new under the sun", came to mind as I worked through the historical accounts of how God's Word was handed down from generation to generation. The historical record showed that Bible translation was an activity of the Church. It has only been in the last hundred years or so that Bible translation became the work of professionally trained individuals.

What I witnessed at the MAST workshop seemed to align more with what I read about the Bible translation efforts during the Reformation than the "traditional approach" of our day. In reading various accounts of Luther's work, I learned that MAST is not fast. In fact, it would be considered slow compared to Luther's timeline or that of his contemporaries. I found it especially interesting that Luther didn't wait on experts to review his work before he released it for public use. He released it early and with the help of friends, he revised it often.

The more I read, the more evident it was that this "new" approach to Bible translation was a lot like the way it had been in the past. I couldn't help remembering what I witnessed at my first MAST event. Ordinary people from the Church were actively engaged with God's Word. It instantly impacted their understanding of God and created a hunger for His Word, a "craving" as Peter described, that they had never experienced before.

Not everyone I talked to responded negatively. I had the privilege of sharing my experiences working with this new approach to Bible translation and how it seemed to fit the historical model with our senior pastor, Dr. Joel Hunter. His response was unexpected yet so encouraging. He said, "This is reformational!"

By May 2018, nearly 1,000 language groups have started Bible translation work using MAST. Several have already finished the New Testament and moved onto translating the Old Testament. I can't help thinking, *the days of spiritual famine for the remaining languages of the world are nearly over. Those who crave the pure milk of the Word will have it in their own language, God's Word in its fullness. All will have the opportunity to "…taste that the Lord is good."*

Prayer

Lord, cause me to crave Your Word that I might grow more in Your salvation.

Lord, accelerate the spread of Your Word to the languages of the world so that all crave Your Word and grow in your salvation.

Chapter Fourteen

Entrusting the Faithful

Verse
...entrust to faithful men, who will be able to teach others also.
2 Timothy 2:2 ESV

Introduction

Was this the *right decision? Is this the job I'm supposed to be doing? Have I missed God's call for my life?* I have asked myself these questions several times in my life. But not when I took the bookkeeping position at NTM's Bible School in Jackson, MI. I was confident that God wanted us to move to Jackson.

Not everyone in our circle of friends shared my confidence. I remember one conversation at the time with a dear friend, "I thought you were going to the Philippines?"

"We were headed in that direction but felt God would have us take a short assignment in Jackson before heading to the field." I said.

"You are a gifted teacher. And the field desperately needs guys like you." He answered me.

"I appreciate the vote of confidence on the teaching. We've only committed to two years here and then we will head to the field." I replied.

He shook his head, "Yeah, I've heard that before. You're here now. You'll never go to the field. It's frustrating when leadership sucks guys like you into these roles."

I thought to myself, *You're wrong. We will go to the field in two years. You'll see!*

As our two-year commitment was nearly complete with the Bible school, friends from Indonesia visited the school encouraging students to consider joining them on the field. Nancy and I were keenly interested in the opportunity especially since she had spent time in Indonesia as a kid with her family. So, I went to see Dave Knapp, the director of the school.

"Dave, is this a good time for a visit?" I asked.

"Sure, come on in. What's on your mind?" He replied.

"You know that we are coming up on our two-year anniversary here at the school. So, we have been thinking about heading to the field. In fact, the presentation today on Indonesia got us wondering if that's where we should go." I said.

"I think Indonesia would be a great place to serve on the field. But, would you consider staying on with us for a longer period?" He asked.

Those words, *you'll never go to the field,* flashed through my mind. "I don't know. Nancy and I have our hearts set on serving overseas." I answered.

"Yes, I know, and I respect that. But here's the reality. If you go, I will need to pull someone else out of training into your role and they won't get to go to the field. You're already trained. And, you're good at book-keeping." He said.

"I appreciate that. But, I'm also a teacher and it seems like God would have me in a teaching role."

"Fair enough. What if we incorporated teaching classes into your role? Would you consider staying on another couple of years?" He asked.

"Give me some time to discuss it with Nancy and I'll let you know." As I left his office, I thought, *Nancy is going to be disappointed.*

When I walked into the apartment, Nancy asked, "Well, how did it go?"

"I think we should sit down for this conversation." I said.

"Okay! Now, what did he say?" She insisted.

"He said that Indonesia was a fine idea. But, he said he would have to pull someone else out of training to take my place if we go. Instead, he would like for us to stay for another couple of years. If we stay, he said the school would add some teaching responsibilities to my role." I replied.

To my surprise she barely hesitated before saying, "I think we should do it."

"Really!" I felt her head and asked, "Are you feeling okay? Who are you and what did you do with my wife?"

"Stop it! You've always wanted to teach here at the Bible school. Another two years isn't that long. I think we should say yes."

We agreed to stay another two years. And, it was a good thing we did! In just a few months' time, Nancy started having serious health issues. Looking back, I can see God's hand in keeping us in the States.

So, I continued to faithfully serve as the school's bookkeeper. And, God used Dave and the other teachers to model Paul's words, "...entrust to faithful men..." as they entrusted me with teaching Christian Ethics, Philippians and Memory classes.

Too Busy

By the time we left the Bible school, I was used to a busy schedule. The school leadership gave me several duties beyond bookkeeping. In addition, I occasionally filled the pulpit for churches in the area, taught junior-high youth at our church, and took classes in pursuit of an accounting degree. It required studies into the evening after the girls went to bed and some time on the weekends. But, I didn't mind the busyness. Studying, teaching, and preaching seemed to energize me.

When we moved to FL, it didn't take long to plug into the ministry at our new church. It was a small group of believers with around 90 to 100 regularly attending. Like most smaller churches, there were several opportunities to get involved. The church needed someone to do the bookkeeping. That seemed like a natural fit since that is what I did every day at NTM headquarters. Nancy and I participated in the Awana program with our girls. I joined the teaching rotation for Sunday school and played guitar for the morning worship service. At one point, I taught Sunday school in the morning, youth group in the evening, directed choir, and filled in for the pastor when he traveled.

Between my duties at NTM and responsibilities at church, it was a busy season of life. So busy, Neal, my father-in-law, pulled me aside one day and said, "Tim, I'm concerned. Have you considered that you might be too busy?"

"Yeah, I'm not going to lie. There are days when I feel a little overwhelmed." I agreed.

"Is there anything you can let go?" He asked.

"I've already stopped participating in the Awana program. That has given me a quiet night at home to study." I replied.

"What about choir? Is that something you could pass on to someone else?" He asked.

"Sure, I could pass that on to someone else. But, listening to the music and preparing through the week refreshes me." I said.

"How about teaching? Could you possibly slow down in that area?" He added.

"That would be hard because I feel energized when I study and teach. Thanks for checking on me. I'll have to give it some more thought."

It was a hard conversation because I liked being busy. Neal was right in suggesting that others could do the things I was doing at church. My work at NTM was important too. I couldn't allow myself to get so busy that it interfered with my duties at work. But, I didn't have to lead choir or teach—I got to do those things! In fact, I felt God wanted me to do those things. And, it gave me a great amount of joy doing them.

While I enjoyed the music and the teaching, Paul's words to Timothy echoed in my mind, "…entrust to faithful men, who will be able to teach others also." Friends had entrusted me with these and other responsibilities. It was time for me to do the same. Instead of holding onto the things I loved to do, I purposed to share the responsibilities with others. For choir, I handed off production responsibilities. Others began making decisions on sound, lighting, sets, and costumes. In Sunday school, I invited another teacher into the rotation. With the youth, we mentored different ones from the group to plan the activities and lead the worship time. Some of the young guys offered to teach some of the lessons. Sharing the responsibilities lightened my load, and instead of feeling like I lost something, I felt joy in seeing others minister.

Anyone Can Do Accounting

Teaching and preaching God's Word has been my passion. It started in that preacher boy contest back in my junior-high school days and has grown through my adult life. Regardless of my job title or life work, God seemed to weave in opportunities to engage in my passion. When I joined NTM, I assumed He wanted me teaching and preaching overseas. I never did make it overseas with NTM. Instead, I took on a support role behind the scenes in finance and accounting. And, as I faithfully served, God gave me the desires of my heart with many teaching opportunities in our local churches.

In 2010, I entered a new season of life. I had been the Vice President of Finance at WA for a couple of years. In that role, some were encouraging me to sit for the CPA exam. The requirements in the State of FL had recently changed. I would need to take additional classes to meet the new requirements. At age 42, I didn't want to drag this process out any longer than necessary. So, I pulled back from all after work activities to devote as much time as possible to acquiring the CPA credential.

It was a good thing that I stepped back from other activities to focus on studying for the exam. It took work! Lots of work! I remember a friend who was also studying for the exam ask me, "Do you know what CPA stands for?"

"Certified Public Accountant!" I responded with a raised eyebrow.

"Wrong! It stands for Can't Pass Again!" He said as he broke into laughter.

"Oh. Now that's hilarious." I said sarcastically.

After I had passed the exam, I remembered thinking to myself, *never again will I do such a crazy thing!* Preparing for that exam was exhausting!

Over the years, I have had a few individuals imply that anyone can do accounting. Actually, it requires a certain set of skills and a commitment to details that might feel unimportant to some. Details that include process and procedures that accounting teams employ to insure the highest levels of integrity when handling financial resources. The procedures are regularly tested and adjusted so that decision-makers can have confidence in the reports they receive and read.

God blessed me with skills for doing accounting. To serve Him faithfully with those skills, I devoted a great deal of time in acquiring and maintaining accounting credentials. But, God also gave me a passion to teach and preach His Word. For a season, I had to set aside the teaching and preaching. It was tough! In that season, I remember wondering *is this what I'm supposed to be doing? Did God really want me focusing all my energy in accounting and finance?* Words that Neal had said to me years before came to my mind, *don't doubt in darkness what you have decided in the light.* I knew God led me to this point and while I couldn't see God's master plan, I knew He had something in mind—something He wanted to entrust me with.

Reviewers Guide

It was official. In September 2012, I passed the CPA exam and received the long-awaited license from the State of FL. It felt good to be done with all that work. For the next few months, I purposed to not take on any extra projects outside of work so I could recover. I thought a less demanding schedule might be refreshing. It wasn't! In fact, I was already wondering *what's next?* I began thinking *it's time to get back to the basics! Back to my passion—studying and teaching Bible!*

I walked over to Bruce's office to ask for some advice. Bruce was my boss and someone I trusted for wise counsel. His door was open. So, I knocked on the door frame as I leaned in and asked, "Is this a good time?"

"Sure, come on in. How can I help?" He asked.

"Well, this is not really work related. It's more of a personal question that I would like to ask."

"Fire away!" He said.

"I've been thinking that it is time for me to refocus on Biblical studies for personal enrichment, and ultimately for an outlet in teaching. You have a doctorate in ministry. Would it be crazy for me to pursue a doctorate in Bible?" I asked.

"First, I don't think it would be crazy. But, I would wonder why? It could look like you are simply trying to pile on more degrees. So, what are you thinking? Why a doctorate in Bible?"

"There is no hiding the fact that I do accounting because God has gifted me to do so. But it is not my passion. I feel the need to study and teach Bible." I said.

"I totally understand what you're saying. Missions has always been my passion. I chose to fly airplanes with Mission Aviation Fellowship to get involved in missions—not because I felt called to fly airplanes." He said.

"Okay! So, what advice would you give me?" I asked.

"My initial thought is that we need to figure out how to build this into your performance goals and make it part of your work. Let me give it some more thought and I will get back with you."

Bruce's response was beyond my expectations. From that conversation, I ended up enrolling in a PhD program with Louisiana Baptist University (LBU) and Bruce worked with me to incorporate my research project into my performance goals for WA. It was the beginning of a new, busy season of life. Unlike the previous season, this one was focused on activities that refreshed and energized me.

I chose LBU's program for a couple of reasons. First, the program included classes with in depth Bible studies like the Gospel of John and Acts and second, Dr. Keeny, the dean of the school called me. It was a joy getting to know Dr. Keeny, as he worked with me to custom-build the program to fit my specific study goals and work objectives. I took the core classes but used the electives as opportunities to complement things we were doing at work. For example, WA was testing computer assisted Bible translation software at the time. So, with Dr. Keeny's coaching, I joined the testing team, worked on the Gospel of Mark, and wrote a paper fulfilling the requirements for an elective.

For my doctoral dissertation, I was required to engage in specific research. This meant spending time in the field observing the work of Bible translation teams and expert consultants. As mentioned earlier, attending MAST workshops forever changed my perspective on Bible translation. I had seen that local believers could do Bible translation with just-in-time training. And they could do it well!

I had also seen highly skilled consultants using a great deal of subjectivity in their checking practices. In one checking session, I remember the consultant reviewing Mark 8 where Jesus asked His disciples, *Who do you say that I am?*

"What was Peter's answer?" The consultant asked.

"Peter said Jesus was the Christ." The translator replied.

"Good. But, Peter didn't really believe it at the time." The consultant went on to say.

After the checking session, I asked the consultant, "So, what was the point in saying Peter didn't believe?"

"They need to understand the full message of the text." He said.

"Okay. But, you seemed to imply that they needed to include that information in their translation of that passage." I said.

"Correct. That would be a more complete translation." He replied.

I was puzzled by this thought and asked another consultant how he would have handled the situation. He gave me a completely different answer. He said, "Some might ascribe to adding information like this to the text. I might have encouraged a footnote or a cross-reference. But I definitely would not have encouraged adding the information about Peter to the text."

From that experience and other similar experiences, I thought *Surely, there must be a more objective way to evaluate Bible translations for accuracy.* One afternoon in May 2017, I had an "ah-ha" moment as Sam, my son-in-law, was in my office explaining to me the latest addition to the MAST process—authentic assessment and rubrics. As he described what those in the education profession clearly understood, it struck me, *this sounds a lot like an audit guide that accountants use when testing the veracity of financial statements.*

In that moment, I sensed that the accounting discipline had something more to offer Bible translation than simply testing financial information and systems. The following month, I assembled a team from multiple disciplines to develop a Reviewer's Guide to Bible translation. Using basic principles from the audit profession, we worked to create objective questions for key passages of Scripture in the New Testament. The sets of questions are designed to determine, "Does the passage clearly communicate the author's intended message?" Yes or no! If yes, the user moves on in the guide. If no, then we included subsequent questions to help users determine what might have caused the deficiency. This guide, like an audit, is designed to help church leaders and translators affirm the quality of their translations or to expose weaknesses.

In less than one year, the team developed, and field tested a guide that church leaders are using today, testing key passages in their translations for accuracy and naturalness.

In one of the early field tests, we demonstrated how to use the guide and within a couple hours, the leaders were testing their translations without our help. When we asked them for feedback, they said, *the questions made us slow down and think about what the text said. It felt like we just had a great Bible study.*

As I listened to their testimonies and feedback, I could only say, *Thank you Lord! Thank you for allowing me, an accountant, the opportunity to empower and "...entrust...faithful men..." to translate Your Word.*

Meaningful Work with Passion

2018 was a year of milestones. Nancy and I celebrated 30 years of marriage, I completed my 10th year with WA, and I turned 50. All special and all significant events! As a bonus, God revealed in a special way how a ministry detour over 25 years ago fit into His plan for my life. He knit everything together—a passion to teach and preach His Word, training to be a church planter, years behind the scenes working in accounting, and now empowering church leaders to translate God's Word.

Life has not gone at all how I imagined it. But looking back, I can see how faithfully serving God and doing what He asked me to do opened opportunities beyond anything I could have asked or dreamed. He amazingly wove together meaningful work in ministry with my passion and heart's desire—teaching and preaching His Word. Now, I get to work with churches and church leaders everywhere empowering them to do Bible translation so that they can have God's Word in its fullness—now and for future generations.

As I look ahead, I know God will continue to use me in ways I can't begin to imagine. I pray that I will continue listening to His leading and faithfully doing the tasks He gives me to do so that in His perfect way I might be part of bringing God's Word in its fullness to others and entrusting them to do the same.

Prayer

God, keep me sensitive to Your leading in my life.

God, keep using me to take Your Word to others in its fullness and to entrust them to do the same.

About the Author

Tim Neu is the Vice President of Finance of Wycliffe Associates (WA). Tim has more than 30 years of experience serving in full time ministry primarily in finance and administration. He trained with Child Evangelism Fellowship as a high school student serving as a summer missionary and entered missionary training with New Tribes Mission (NTM) immediately following high school to prepare for life in foreign missions. Tim served with NTM for 16 years in several different roles including branch bookkeeper, office manager, director of operations, and CFO. He has been with WA for over 10 years providing oversight in areas of finance, corporate structure, technology, and most recently translation services. Tim holds two bachelor's degrees, an MBA, a PhD in Biblical studies, and is a licensed CPA.

Tim and his wife Nancy live in Orlando, Florida. They have two daughters, two sons-in-law, and four grandchildren.